Sundays

with

Ron Rozelle

Sundays With Ron Rozelle

by Ron Rozelle

TCU Press
Fort Worth, Texas

Library of Congress Cataloging-in-Publication Data

Rozelle, Ron, 1952-
Sundays with Ron Rozelle / by Ron Rozelle.
p. cm.
ISBN 978-0-87565-390-7
1. Oakwood (Tex.)–Social life and customs–Anecdotes. 2. Texas–
Social life and customs–Anecdotes. 3. City and town life–Texas–
Oakwood--Anecdotes. 4. Rozelle, Ron, 1952---Anecdotes. 5.
Oakwood (Tex.)–Biography–Anecdotes. I. Title.
F394.O255R69 2009
976.4'233–dc22
                    2008034474

TCU Press
P. O. Box 298300
Fort Worth, Texas 76129
817.257.7822
http://www.prs.tcu.edu

To order books: 800.826.8911

Designed and linocut illustration by
Barbara Mathews Whitehead

Photograph of author, courtesy of Karen Rozelle

To Karen, Diane, Janie & Thomas,

and Suzy & David.

Good traveling companions.

Contents

Foreword

Long ago, when I was a boy, I used to go with my father to the lumberyard he managed in a small Central Texas town. And on winter days, carpenters and customers would wander in, choose a cane-bottomed chair around the pot-bellied office stove, and stay for a bit to talk—about the weather, about a job they were working on, about the minister's Sunday sermon, about sick livestock (almost everyone in those days had a family cow), about hunting trips, about their children's feats or snags at school, about politics on every level. Everything and anything was the subject, wherever the paths of conversation might lead.

It was a kind of easy, unhurried discourse that's been lost in today's world, where speed dictates and too much information is too quickly pumped out to all kinds of electronic gadgets to assault eyes and ears, frustrating proper contemplation. The mind needs a little time to think about the ordinary highs and lows of everyday life.

So, welcome Ron Rozelle. In these easy essays filled with humor and wisdom, he gently guides readers through a year's worth of subjects—from the pervasive presence of cell phones to the assuring sound and sight of the annual migration of geese, from the incalculable value of family dogs and cats to the enticing Thanksgiving aromas of pecan and sweet potato pies—that one might otherwise think unimportant. In his hands, they become meaningful, if not momentous, stimulating thoughts that might have slumbered without his reminders.

I wager that you'll relish and remember this comfortable journey that takes you nowhere in particular, yet everywhere, to learn nothing specifically, yet everything.

—Robert Compton
former book review editor,
The Dallas Morning News

Preface

Bill Cornwell, publisher of the *Brazosport Facts*—the daily paper in my town—and I meet once a year for lunch; usually he buys. These rituals consist of his wanting to know what current book I am working on and me anxious to hear about whatever local topics are hot at the time. But a couple of lunches ago, Bill and I agreed that it might not be such a horrible idea for me to try my hand at a weekly column.

He said I could take on any topic that suited me, as long as the pieces were short—hovering between 700 and 800 words—not particularly controversial and, hopefully, interesting enough to entice the reader to come back for more occasionally.

For my part, I saw a fine opportunity to stretch my writing muscles. I was, at the time of that meeting, just beginning a big novel involving a hit man, redemption, detailed back stories, and more rough and tumble action than I had tackled in six previous books. It would take a year to write it, I figured, and the prospect of putting that heavy project aside once a week and letting my imagination wander to wherever it happened to go seemed like just the ticket.

It has proven to be so. I've very much enjoyed visiting with readers about these columns that popped up in their Sunday papers, collected here in chronological order and covering a full calendar year—beginning in late July—and a bit more. Each one is, of course, from my perspective and mine alone, and in each I have tried to adhere to a short catalog of ground rules that I set forth in the initial piece.

Robert Frost, in his famous poem "The Pasture" starts by saying he is going out to do some not very important things and might stop to look at things around him along the way. He concludes with "you come, too."

Whether or not the following pieces deal with anything important is a matter of opinion. I've followed my fancy and have most certainly made countless stops on this enjoyable journey to peruse, ponder, and perhaps pontificate.

My invitation is the same as Mr. Frost's.

You come, too.

Sundays with Ron Rozelle

A cup of coffee

Today marks the inaugural installment of this new adventure, whatever it turns out to be. And right here, amid the news, good and bad, and the sports scores, amid who got married and who died, who wrote a letter to the editor, and what Dagwood and Blondie are up to, I hope you'll find a few minutes for it every week.

I like to think of this as our having a cup of coffee together to start our day, or one in the evening to finish it, dependent on when you read the paper. Back in Oakwood, the little East Texas burg where I was raised, having a cup of coffee with friends was a treasured event. The men would have theirs at Laurene's Café, while ladies met around each other's breakfast tables. Often the problems of the world were tackled. And I don't buy into the notion that it was a simpler world then, with simpler problems. As I recall, the Kennedy assassination, the Vietnam War, and racial discrimination weren't exactly petty trifles. Every age has its own problems, I guess, sufficient to itself.

But mostly those conversations over cups of coffee dealt with less significant things. Recipes were shared. Sick friends were discussed and put on one another's prayer lists. Somebody got a new color television set, and it turned out that Ed Sullivan looked even worse than he did in black and white. Cattle prices were up, or down.

These assemblies transpired at any time during the day and sometimes several times daily. Whenever friends wanted to confer about anything, specific or general.

And that's just what I'd like for this to be.

There's no telling what our subject will be on any given Sunday. We'll be fancy free and will wander in whatever direction the wind and current events take us.

Let's steer clear, if you don't mind, of religion—I'll hold to my religion and you hold to yours—but we'll probably take up faith in general as our topic now and again. We'll leave politics to the syndicated pundits and angry letter writers, unless, that is, some politician does something either interesting or aggravating, the latter being the most likely case. Endorsements, implied or explicit, of anyone running for any office in any place will never be offered. Good, old-fashioned patriotism is allowed, but I'll keep it shy of soapbox bellowing.

I teach senior English and creative writing in high school, so I'll talk about teachers and students and education now and then. I might as well go on record right now as believing that good teachers are underpaid, bad teachers should find another career, students are smarter and have more potential than they are sometimes given credit for, and the giving over of a school's curriculum to the teaching of a single state test is both dangerous and wrong.

I'll talk about books occasionally, since I do dearly love reading good books and see it as an enterprise that society should take up more in earnest. I am in the business of writing books, but I'll refrain from pushing them at you, like a barker at a sideshow. And Oakwood, my little hometown, will make regular appearances, since you couldn't any more take that little town out of me than you could train a cat to roll over.

Speaking of cats. My wife Karen and I are empty nesters now, with the exception of four cats named Will and Grace, Earl Gray, and Missy. We're awfully attached to them and pretty much let them run the place. But I promise to not go on and on about them like some tiresome people do about pets and children.

In fact, you might never hear another word from me about those cats.

But, then again, you might.

On wizards

Many people—what pollsters would label a "significant demographic group"—find young readers' fascination with the *Harry Potter* novels to be dangerous, disturbing, and indicative of a societal slide into regions dark and dire. And most, if not all, of their conclusion rests solely on the fact that Harry, the baby-faced lad in the large eyeglasses, is, in fact, a wizard.

My first inclination here is to suggest that this group find something more important to worry about. But, after all, it isn't any of my business what people choose to worry about. Also, I'm well aware that their concerns are, in many cases, born of deeply held beliefs, religious and moral, and who am I to trample around in that field? I harbor pretty deep religious and moral beliefs myself, and I don't take kindly to any such trampling.

So what I would suggest is this: consider the fact that kids, millions of them, are spending time, when enjoying the *Harry Potter* adventures, reading big thick books. And that, I have to believe, just can't be all bad. After all, they could be up to no good on the Internet, or watching hours and hours of reality shows on television, or racking up body counts in video games, or yakking on the cell phones that seem, these days, to be surgically attached to their heads.

To my dying day, I will be an advocate of the importance of reading. Even about wizards.

Before Harry, wizardry didn't seem to have been viewed as such an evil enterprise. The Wizard of Oz, remember, wasn't a bad man (just a bad wizard, as he told Dorothy upon being found out). And many venerable ladies who find great fault in young Mr. Potter and other fantasy tales wouldn't, I suspect, at all mind being called a "wizard in the kitchen." One of the most famous science teachers of all time was television's Mr. Wizard, who stirred things up in test tubes and captured the attention of American children at a time when sparkling clean programs like *Leave it to Beaver* and *Father Knows Best* were the standards for home and hearth. Nobody, even in that Eisenhower utopia, objected to Mr. Wizard or to his title. (I must confess that I was not a Mr. Wizard devotee, being not at all bent toward science or math. I was much more of a Captain Kangaroo man, finding dancing bears and tennis ball-tossing rabbits more in tune with my world view).

Several years ago, a student in my high school creative writing class wrote a story in which the central character was an old wizard complete, I think I recall, with a pointed hat (perhaps with stars and slivers of moons on it; I can't remember), a dark robe, a wand, and scowling features. The old fellow's name was Ellezor. A name which, I thought at first reading flowed smoothly on the page and was an altogether fitting name for a wizard. I probably scribbled that in the margin, since I am a constant margin scribbler. When students started giggling during the silent reading of the piece, I asked what I had missed.

Ellezor, it turns out, is my last name spelled backwards.

It stuck. And I even began signing occasional memos to my independent studies writers as Ellezor. I never donned a robe or a pointed hat, but I'm sure that at least a few taxpayers would find something to carp about in my identifying myself in a public schoolroom as a wizard. If those folks gave their imaginations free rein, as naysayers often do, it wouldn't be long till they envisioned boiling kettles, dead cats, and crystal balls. None of which would fit in my classroom even if I wanted them to, since it is overflowing with books and manuscripts and computers.

So, to anyone who might be concerned, I will say this:

I am not a wizard, though I do sometimes play one in class. If I were one, I would use my powers for good and would turn the world into a better place, with no war, no murders, no prejudice, no starving children. I would wave my magic wand around enough times to make people tolerant of others' viewpoints and supportive of their children's interest in reading, as long as the reading material is not truly harmful. I would conjure up long, productive, happy lives for every student I teach and would make the Astros win the World Series.

But I am not a wizard. So be not afraid. And have a nice day.

—Ellezor (occasionally)

Another piece of the puzzle falls into place

Red Buttons died a couple of weeks ago. And I was sad when I read it in the paper.

It wasn't that Mr. Buttons—who many readers will be too young to know anything about, and others too forgetful to remember—had been one of my particular favorites among actors or comedians. But he kept popping up here and there along the way. The first time being when he hosted a weekly program that came on one of the three channels that we got on the big Zenith in the house I grew up in. If the weather was clear and the atmosphere conductive between our tall antenna and Dallas, then we could watch Red Buttons dance that silly dance of his. We watched Red Skelton do his silly dances on some other night, and I was probably a teenager before I realized that not all people named Red were clowns.

I recall that Buttons dressed flashy for that show, with a handsome bowtie not too unlike the one that my mother snapped onto me some Sunday mornings before we went to church. Mine was green, I think; Red's was any color I imagined it to be since it was a black and white television.

Later, I enjoyed him in movies. Like *Hatari!*, *They Shoot Horses, Don't They?*, *Pete's Dragon*, and the original *Poseidon Adventure*. If you want to watch one fine job of acting, rent *Sayonara*, the Marlon Brando flick with Buttons playing a G.I. who falls in love with a Japanese girl. In Japan. Right after World

War II. That performance spoke volumes about racial prejudice in an age when almost everybody either avoided the issue or opened their mouths and made fools of themselves. It won Buttons a best supporting actor Oscar, and in all probability made a lasting impression on at least one little boy in deep East Texas about bigotry.

Years later, when I visited the beaches of Normandy on the fiftieth anniversary of the D-Day landings, I looked up at the steeple of the old church in Sainte Mère Église, half expecting to see him still hanging there by his parachute. Such was the impact of his performance in *The Longest Day* that there actually *was* a parachute up there, with a mannequin dressed like the paratrooper that Buttons portrayed.

So, there he's always been, present and accounted for somewhere in the periphery of my consciousness, this small, lively man who used to dance for me when I was a child, and provided entertainment and a few laughs occasionally. I never saw him in person. Never wrote him a fan letter. Never thought much about him one way or another beyond the time I spent watching him perform.

And now he's dead. And I was a little sad when I learned of it.

Every time somebody whose name I've known my entire life slips away—like Red Buttons and, just a day or two before him, June Allyson—it's like a tiny piece of the big puzzle clicks irrevocably into place. It occurs to me that some of the old movies I watch on AMC are peopled entirely by performers who are no longer with us. That's a bit disconcerting, don't you think? And it lends itself to weighty musings regarding the meaning of life and its brevity.

And before you write in to explain these feelings I'm having to me, let me assure you that I'm pretty sure I understand what's going on. The world is changing. I'm getting older. It's best to just get on with it and roll with the flow.

On the day that I read about Red Buttons's death, I dug out my DVD of *Hatari!* and watched him chase animals around Africa with John Wayne (dead) and Bruce Cabot (also dead), all of them vibrantly alive for the length of that movie. All of them part of a past that, rightly or wrongly, seems golden in retrospect.

But, let's not forget what Robert Frost, that wise old New England poet (dead, of course) told us.

Nothing gold can stay.

Letters

Have you gotten a letter lately?

Not an e-mail. Or a text message. Not a note scribbled out by someone in a hurry. Or even a formal business letter, which was more than likely signed by a computer. I'm talking about a personal, handwritten letter with a salutation, a proper closing, and an actual signature.

Me, neither.

I used to get them all the time. I used to *write* them all the time. I've got, on a shelf in my closet, an old shoebox crammed full with letters that came to me during my army days at a little base in Germany, where I personally kept democracy secure.

Many of the residents of Oakwood—the little East Texas hamlet that, along with my parents, collectively raised me— wrote to me regularly. Some good-hearted souls even sent care packages. Miss Eudie Belle Cutler sent a nine-layer jam cake with a different homemade jam between each layer. But mostly it was just letters that arrived at Mail Call. And that was fine with me. Those letters eased the homesickness that was pretty strong in a young fellow who had never even ridden an airplane before Uncle Sam sent his greetings.

I have, in my bookcases, several fat volumes of famous people's collected letters. I enjoy reading what Ernest Hemingway wrote to his various wives. And Steinbeck's daily letters to his editor during the writing of *East of Eden*—all of them grouped into an amazing book called *Journal of a Novel*—were more beneficial to me as a novelist than any writer's manual could have been.

In the high school where I've taught for the last twenty-five years, building up that enormous state pension that I'm going to take them up on one of these days, there was, until recent renovations, an interesting display consisting of twenty or so copies of historical documents on laminated plaques in the main entryway.

One of them was a handwritten letter from President Franklin Roosevelt to Joseph Stalin, informing him that "the immediate appointment of General Eisenhower to command of Overlord operation has been decided upon." Beneath it was another short, scribbled note—from General Marshall to Eisenhower—which says "I thought you might like to have this for your mementos."

I'll just bet he did, don't you?

I've always found it both fascinating and fitting that the handing over of the biggest invasion force in the history of the world was transacted in a few handwritten lines.

I don't know when letter writing fell almost completely by the wayside as an important and common human enterprise. Probably it began its slide when e-mailing came into vogue, which lets us dash off truncated communications without any regard to spelling, capitalization, or grammar. Then the final death knell must have been with the advent of text messaging on cell phones. My goodness, when you can quickly tap out the bare bone essentials you need to impart, why would you pour a bit of your heart into a multi-page letter, address an envelope, and be out the cost of a stamp?

I can tell you why.

Occasionally, I take down that box of letters I got when I was in the army. All of them are fun to read again, but the real treasures are the ones from my parents and from my two sisters. When I hold a letter from my mother in my hands, rub the brittle pages between my fingers, and decipher her tiny, wandering hen-scratch handwriting, it's almost like she's back with me for a few minutes.

I don't have a box of old e-mails. Or text messages. Because not enough effort is put into them to last. And almost never is enough of the writer's soul infused into them to be worth keeping.

So, sit right down and write someone a letter. The recipient will feel better for it.

And so will you.

Good Daddies

Let me tell you about Mackenzie, my grandniece out in Southern California, who is lucky enough to have been granted a good Daddy. Maybe you share the same good fortune. I hope so.

It would be wonderful if all fathers were good Daddies. But spending any time at all reading the paper or watching the news on television provides conclusive evidence to the contrary. There are far too many men out there who just aren't up to the job. And that's a shame.

Mackenzie had an excellent Daddy, by all accounts. I never met Jim, since Southern California is pretty far out of my regular range, and since he and my niece Lisa decided to live apart not long after their only child was born. But Mackenzie, a beautiful and vibrant thirteen year old that laughs at my jokes (as reliable an indicator of intelligence and worth as I've come across), was the link that held the little family together anyway. Mackenzie cemented a strong, dependable friendship between Jim and Lisa who, having created something wonderful together, decided to see the project all the way through as a team.

A little over a week ago, while Mackenzie and her mother were in Hawaii for a holiday before the school year started, Jim was involved in a freak motorcycle accident. They barely made it home in time for Mackenzie to stand by her father's hospital bed to say goodbye before the life support machine was turned off.

Lisa was only six when her own father was killed in a car accident. Lisa is the oldest child of my oldest sister Diane, so I was only five when she was born, and I had a devil of a time figuring out just what our relationship was. At one point, I was pretty sure that I was her grandfather. I wasn't, apparently, the sharpest knife in the drawer as a child.

Anyway, Lisa and I have always been more like brother and sister than uncle and niece. And I hurt badly for her and her daughter when we got the news last week. I couldn't get the image out of my mind of her at her own Daddy's funeral so long ago, five months before President Kennedy was killed. Lisa was a skinny little thing, rather tomboyish and out of her element in a dress, having to stand by her mother and listen to some old woman tell them both that this was all for the best. And I had to wonder—and still do—how that could possibly be right.

Nothing, to my way of thinking, about strong, good people dying in their prime is for the best. But it does happen. And people cry, and grieve, and maybe get angry. But then, being people, they get up and go on with the business of living. It's difficult, and sometimes darned near impossible, but it's part of the beauty of how we're put together as people.

We can do it.

Losing one of the people who gave her life is one of the hardest things Mackenzie will likely ever have to endure. My own father died when I was a lot older than her, and when he was a lot older than Jim, but it was still a staggeringly difficult thing to go through. Any way you look at it, letting go of someone as essential as a father is just downright heartbreaking.

But here's the good part, if there is one.

If he was a good Daddy, then something almost magical occurs, because it turns out that he's not really gone at all. As time goes by, he pops up pretty often in your memories and your thinking and your wondering. For the rest of your life.

In time, Mackenzie will be fine. Her family loves her very much, and will be right there with her. For high school. And college. To watch her walk down the aisle, if that's what she wants to do. To watch her grow into the amazing woman that she will become.

And part of her Daddy will be there, too.

Because he was a good Daddy.

A useful book

Last winter as I was reading *Katherine Graham's Washington*, the late *Washington Post* matriarch's collection of various authors' essays about the capital city and its history, I came across an excerpt from an old book that means a lot to me. It's called *Starling of the White House*, the story of Colonel E. W. Starling, a Secret Service agent who protected presidents Woodrow Wilson through Franklin Roosevelt. It was one of the very first books I ever read.

My mother had brought it to Oakwood, our little East Texas town, along with several hundred other volumes from the leftover inventory of the book shop she ran in the front room of her parents' house in Livingston during and just after the Second World War. My father, home from the South Pacific and back in his position as the superintendent of the Oakwood schools, had swept her off her feet and up into the country, along with all those books. A few years later, after I had made my grand entrance, I pulled *Starling* down from the shelf and commenced what would become a lifetime of reading.

At the supper table, I recounted the heroic deeds of the brave Colonel to my parents and bored sister and stated my intention of becoming a Secret Service agent myself one day. Everyone managed not to laugh and, needless to say, I didn't follow through on the plan. I doubt my parents took that career goal very seriously, but they never advised against it. If any American boy could grow up to be a president, I guess they figured, then he had the equal right to become the protector of presidents.

The next time I pulled the book down was nearly forty years later, when my old friend and college roommate Jim Willett, the retired warden of the Walls prison unit in Huntsville, asked me to help him with his memoirs. I had no idea how to go about writing another man's story in *my* voice. And then I remembered that was exactly what the author of *Starling of the White House*, Thomas Sugrue, had done with the Colonel's life.

I revisited the introduction by Sugrue, in which he set forth his goal of getting into his subject's head and relating the events in first person, as if Starling were telling him the story over a glass of iced tea on the front porch. And, after reading the entire book again, that is exactly what I did with *Warden*, down to prefacing it with a chapter of my own in which I introduce Willett, myself, and the prison and then get myself completely off the stage before Jim's story begins.

So *Starling*, its pages brittle and brown as autumn leaves, served me well a second time. It's a solid yarn—too old fashioned for many modern readers, I imagine, who are given to plots splashed out quickly, with plenty of sex and violence and foul language the Colonel wouldn't have abided. *Starling of the White House* is about a good man with a hard job, who was humble, quiet, courteous, brave, and altogether devoted to his duty and to the nation that he loved dearly. Virtues that some cynics would say are difficult to locate in modern society. But I suspect they aren't, if you look hard enough. In fact, I found them all alive and well in my buddy Jim Willett.

I suspect, too, that if any of those things ended up in *me*— which is arguable, at best—it is at least partly because I found that book and read it so long ago. Good writing, especially about good lives, has a way of rubbing off on readers. I'm glad of that.

I'm confident that I'll read *Starling of the White House* again once or twice, maybe several times, before I'm done with reading for good. And I recommend it to you. It was published in 1946 by Simon and Schuster, and you'll have to search pretty hard for it. It's out of print.

But it shouldn't be.

Thank you very much, Mr. Schieffer, and goodbye

Do you want to know who I really like on television right now? Bob Schieffer. On the *CBS Evening News*.

I should preface this by telling you that my liking anything on television is pretty much the kiss of death. Since anything I like usually gets cancelled quickly. And, sure enough, Mr. Schieffer is retiring to make way for Katie Couric to complete her much heralded migration over from NBC.

I'm not a big fan of Mr. Schieffer because he delivers the news any better than the people on the other networks; they all seem adept at keeping me up to snuff on war and pestilence and moral decline. Or even because he's a Texan, like Rather and Cronkite before him. Time moves on and we knew that sooner or later we'd have to relinquish that honor.

Bob Schieffer gets my vote as the best news anchor on the air because he practices something every evening that seems to be going completely out of style. Something that many people would consider a trivial matter indeed. But when it disappears completely it will be a sad day for us all.

I'm talking about common courtesy.

When a correspondent pops up on the big monitor beside Schieffer and makes his or her spiel, Bob always makes it a point to thank them when they're done. Sometimes he even says

"Thank you, Sally (or Robert or whoever). Thank you *very* much." With emphasis on the "very."

And it comes across, at least to me, that he means it.

How many times have you been thanked by a cashier or the kid in the drive-through at a fast food place or any number of other people with whom you come into contact, and you instinctively know that they don't mean it. That those two little words are nothing more than that: two words. They might as well be saying "off with you, now. We're done here."

More often than not, "thank yous" are tossed out like beads off a Mardi Gras float, signifying nothing.

Even more irksome, to me at least, is what has become the common response to a statement of gratitude. Once upon a time, and not so very long ago, if you said "thank you" to someone, you could bet the farm that they would come back with "you're welcome." Which is, in itself, a term of endearment. It means "it was my gift, and you are most welcome to it."

I've been conducting a little private poll for the last couple of years. Every time I tell a waiter or waitress—or anyone else—"thank you," I pay close attention to their response. And it saddens me to report that it is almost always—I'd guess somewhere around 80 percent—"no problem." Which, if you think about it, verges on being a negative statement. It can't mean anything other than "It's okay. You managed to not pose a difficulty this time." Which is a far cry from "you're welcome."

While I've got my steam up, let me go ahead and take on another pet peeve in this general category. "Goodbye," the statement used down the long centuries when parting, has almost invariably become "later." "Goodbye", if you look it up (I did) is a condensed version of "God be with you." It is a blessing, and a particularly beautiful one at that. While "later," its universally fashionable proxy, is nothing more than a postponement.

I hate to think where we're headed with this gradual downslide from courteous communication to curt, snippy ways to blow each other off. Before long, we'll be shouting out all manner of scurrilous disparagements at our meetings and our partings. And the world will slip a little further toward folly and pandemonium.

So, thank you, Bob Schieffer, for your commendable behavior. Please leave a memo for Katie Couric to keep up the good work.

Because I think that we—as a thinking, caring society—should be nicer to each other, even in the most trivial of situations. That's my opinion, and now I'll say goodbye.

And I mean it.

September eleventh

Tomorrow is, of course, the universally definitive date for the current generation. It's a member of a very small, very exclusive club. December 7, 1941. November 22, 1963.

And September 11, 2001.

No American who was alive and sufficiently alert to grasp the situation that day will likely ever forget where they were when they heard the news. Neither will they forget the image of those two tall, beautiful buildings—symbols of our ingenuity and our daring—gushing out smoke and flames. Nor the horror of them crashing down, one floor into the next, finally into what would enter into our language as ground zero. Which is sacred ground in our consciousnesses, our memory, and our collective soul.

For my generation, another ground zero is Dealy Plaza, stretching out beneath the Texas School Book Depository in Dallas. Not because one man died there, but because we all changed there. After that autumn morning, the horrors that followed it—the murders of Martin Luther King, Jr. and Bobby Kennedy, the deaths of student protestors at Kent State, and other atrocities—hit us with a numbing that was more sadness than shock.

On that long ago November day, my father, the superintendent of our little country school, told us all of President Kennedy's death over the intercom. After school, my mother drove me to Palestine, twenty miles away, for a dentist appointment. Half way there, with news of the nation's grief on the car radio, she pulled our Impala off the road, leaned over the big steering wheel, and started crying.

Not knowing what to do, I sat on my side of the wide seat and watched her. I was probably wondering why she was crying for a man she had neither seen in person nor even voted for.

I don't have to wonder now. She was crying for all of us. She was weeping for a world where such a thing could happen.

A little over twenty years before that day, my father learned of the Pearl Harbor attack over the radio on a Sunday morning. And that far away naval base in the middle of the Pacific became ground zero for his generation. He was, even back then, the superintendent. And he'd be away for the duration of the ensuing war, aided by the daily prayers of the children in the Oakwood school who asked for his safe return, not because of any great devotion to my father but because they didn't care for the old man who was dug out of retirement to fill in for him.

Five years ago tomorrow, I was in the throws of severe back spasms. In fact, Karen and I were at the doctor's office when we heard that the two buildings had collapsed. I spent the rest of that day propped up in a chair, slipping in and out of a groggy, drug-induced shadowland. Every time I surfaced for long enough to bring the television into focus, I wondered if the images I was see-ing could possibly be happening. And every time, before I slipped away again, I realized that the world really had gone mad outside my living room.

One of those shots on TV showed a woman on a street in New York. The smoke from ground zero rose up behind her, clutter and debris lay all around, and she was crying like my mother had cried on that November afternoon when I was eleven. This woman didn't appear to have been injured; her clothes weren't soiled or torn and she wasn't bandaged. So she obviously wasn't a literal survivor of the unbelievable carnage.

Nonetheless, she was a survivor in the sense that this had happened in her city. In her country. On her planet.

And she was crying.

Today, on the eve of the anniversary of that sacrilege, we are all survivors. Each and every one of us.

And the highest tribute that we can pay to those who perished is exactly the same one paid in 1941 and 1963. It is, in fact, the only tribute that is in our capacity to offer.

We can remember.

A tale of a tale unappealing in New York

My friend Dean Smith lives on a pretty hilltop out between Graham and Breckenridge where he raises longhorn cattle and remembers a life full of adventures that most of the rest of us can only dream about.

Dean was a state champion high school trackster, a star footballer and runner at The University of Texas, won a gold medal at the 1952 Summer Olympics in Helsinki, and was drafted by the Los Angeles Rams in 1957. Not bad for a skinny kid raised by his grandmother during a depression, who sold eggs from the hen yard so he could go to the Gene Autry flicks in Breckenridge on Saturdays.

At the end of the preseason with the Rams, Coach Sid Gilman called him in and told him to pack his bags because he had been traded to Pittsburgh. Then Dean told him that he didn't have any interest in moving to Pennsylvania—that he'd only agreed to play at all to be close to the big movie studios. His dream, you see, was to work in western films.

The organization took pity on such a unique case and let him out of his contract. Then Dean drove his brand new car—with all the payments yet to be made and no income with which to pay them—over to Warner Brothers studio. He had a friend, Jim Baumgarner, who worked there who had promised to help him hire on in the industry.

At the gate, the guard looked though his list three times before telling Dean that there was no Baumgarner on the payroll. That his buddy must have been pulling his leg.

Confused and dejected, Dean drove back to his grandmother's house outside of Graham, where he moped around for several days. Until the Sunday *Dallas Morning News* plopped into the yard. And there, splashed all over the cover of *Parade* magazine was a color photo of his buddy Jim Baumgarner, whose name had been changed to James Garner. This explained that confused gate guard. The article inside said that Garner was at the State Fair in Dallas that weekend to promote a new movie and Dean told his grandmother that he intended to drive over there and see him.

At that point, most grandmothers that I have known would have told him that the wise thing to do would be to get himself back out to California and beg Coach Gilman for that football job back. But this one looked Dean square in the eyes and said she figured he'd better go see his friend. That, if he didn't, he would spend the rest of his life wondering what would have happened if he had.

Garner pulled a string or two and launched Dean into a career as a stunt man and actor that would last over forty years. It was while working on *The Alamo* that he got to know John Wayne, with whom he would remain close friends until the Duke's death. He worked on ten pictures with Wayne in addition to many others with some of the biggest names in Hollywood. He did everything from being killed by James Caan in *El Dorado*, to doubling Robert Duvall in *True Grit*, Robert Redford in *Jeremiah Johnson*, and even Maureen O'Hara in *McLintock!*. He taught Paul Newman how to jump hurdles for *Cat on a Hot Tin Roof* and was Goldie Hawn's dialogue coach for *The Sugar Land Express*.

Last year, Dean and I worked up a proposal for a book about his amazing life. Jim Garner agreed to write the introduction. So far, New York editors have maintained that there's not enough readers out there interested in John Wayne or old movies and that our book would be a gamble.

It won't come as a surprise to you that I wholeheartedly disagree. I believe that Dean's story would find plenty of readers. Not because of my writing, but because of the life he's lived. And the man he is.

By the way, Dean's third big celebrity rodeo benefiting the John Wayne Cancer Institute will bust out of the gates in Abilene soon. I'm recommending it to everybody.

Except those New York editors.

When qualifiers
become warnings,
watch out

Let's spend a few minutes on the subject of warnings, good and evil.

Some warnings are warnings outright, like "Dangerous Curves Ahead" and "Mean Dog in Yard," which provide useful information to drivers, and burglars. Then there is the classic sign on a park bench: "Wet Paint." The disregarding of which would have you walking around in horizontal stripes, looking like a convict in an old movie.

I'm as appreciative as the next guy of a well-intended warning, even when it is given in the guise of general information. In the school where I teach, the good ladies in the cafeteria used to put up a sign occasionally. It was hand-lettered and said "Liver on Thursday." Now, people who actually enjoyed consuming filtration organs might have appreciated knowing when they would be available. But the rest of us knew what the cafeteria ladies were up to. After all, they never posted notices announcing when meat loaf or fish sticks would be served. We knew that the little sign was a warning, so that most of us could pack a lunch on Thursday. We called it the Liver Alert.

So, a specific heads-up about a situation is fine with me. But when folks insert little hidden caveats, little qualifiers in anticipation of what they are about to do, that's when my internal alarm starts clanging.

Like this one: "I'm not prejudiced, but . . ." invariably means that the speaker is about to say something hideously prejudicial or tell a racist story or joke. Incidentally, it also indicts him as exactly what he just proclaimed himself not to be.

It's like those little blurbs that some novelists put at the front of their books. You know the one: "This is a work of fiction, and any similarity to any person living or dead is purely coincidental." Which we all know really means "I'm about to put some people that I know in here and give them different names to protect myself in case they have good lawyers."

Both phrases—the "I'm not prejudiced but . . ." and the "This is a work of fiction . . ."—never fool anybody. They're just devious snippets we employ to cover our tracks and a certain part of our anatomy.

Here's the one that rankles me the most. "I tell it like it is." Whenever someone says that, they may be attesting that they will be telling the truth, which is good. But more often than not, they might as well say "I tend to be brutally blunt because I am too self-centered or ignorant or just plain mean to care a fig about anyone else's feelings."

I've heard some mighty hurtful things get trotted out after "I tell it like it is." And the speaker always seems to feel vindicated in causing the hurt, as if that one little phrase provides carte blanche, a boundless license to slash someone up like a sofa in a room full of cats.

I don't know about you, but it seems to me that people don't always need to be told a thing like it "is." A child who misses a high fly ball doesn't need to hear from his coach or his buddies that he's just no good at this, that he couldn't catch a cold, that he should take up some hobby where skill is not a requirement. What he really needs to hear, when he comes back in to the dugout, is how he gave it his best shot. How bright the sun is this afternoon. How everybody misses one occasionally.

That kid will get enough reality in his lifetime, enough "telling it like it is."

Warnings that keep folks from making mistakes are blessings. But qualifiers that are intended as nothing more than disclaimers for the purpose of legitimizing crude or cruel behavior ought to be outlawed in a society seeking to behave correctly.

They're as distasteful, to me at least, as a serving of liver.

Our state fair

When our youngest daughter Megan was in the first grade I tried to tell her about Big Tex. Who is, for you new arrivals to the Lone Star State and you natives who just haven't paid proper attention, the giant cowboy who stands sentinel at the State Fair in Dallas every autumn.

We were planning a trip up to Dallas and I saw Megan as my only chance to convey what Big Tex and the fair really meant. I figured her two sisters, just three and five years older than her, were already too worldly to get it. Their attention had already wandered off toward boys and pop music. So Megan was my one shot.

Just as she was the only one I could bribe to watch *Monday Night Football* with me. The deal being that she would get a mini Snickers bar every time her chosen team scored in the first half before she had to go to bed.

Megan's all grown up now, with a college degree, battling Houston traffic every day to get to and from a real job, and cooking whole meals without calling to ask how to do it. I doubt that she even remembers that long ago trip to Dallas. But I do.

When I told her about the fair, I had attempted to relay to her what it had meant to me when I was her age—when my parents and my sister and I would stay with Uncle Gaston and Aunt Billie and ride the city bus out to Fair Park. I would scan the tops of trees and light poles from the bus for any evidence of the big Ferris wheel, or the great, curved rim of the Cotton Bowl, or the tower of the Electric Building. Then, standing at the little picket fence that surrounded Big Tex, there would be that moment of pure joy peppered with a little fear when I looked hard into his painted eyes and listened to his deep voice.

I had known, of course, that the voice was the voice of a real man hidden away somewhere with a microphone. I might not have been the brightest crayon in the box, but I wasn't the village idiot, either. I had known that he was frame and chicken wire and cable covered with plaster, and that someone pulled the cable that made the big mouth work (only the bottom lip moved—like a bad cartoon). Nevertheless, he used to hold me spellbound.

When we took Megan and her sisters there, Big Tex didn't look nearly so big; in fact, they paid hardly any attention to him at all. I guess they saw him for what he was. Only I could see him for what I remembered him being.

Even Megan, on whom I had expended all that time and phi-losophy, seemed unimpressed. I should have brought along a bag of mini Snickers.

Young folks and people who didn't go to the fair in the old days go now at a disadvantage, I believe. For they have no way of knowing the old magic of the place. Once, it was a magnet, all glitter and bright lights, which called to it people from sand farms and rich river bottoms and cities and towns. The fact that it existed at all gave credibility to long, back-breaking days spent in fields and factories. Those were mostly people of the land and of industry. And if a whole fair was given over to those things, then their lives surely must have had value, and their efforts must have been essential.

They came every year and brought with them the proof of their efforts: fattened hogs and corn-fed calves and perfect pies and jellies and such. Once there, they would wander around the shiny new cars and farm implements, taste the samples of free food—like the miniature loaves of Mrs. Baird's bread that my sister Janie and I liked the best—and would try their hand at the games of chance along the midway, wasting a few precious coins and not begrudging the waste.

They'd eat corny dogs and cotton candy and roasting ears slathered in butter, then give it all a good shaking up on the Tilt-a-Whirl. Then they'd watch a red-golden North Texas sunset from atop the biggest roller coaster anywhere.

It's probably still a great state fair, as Rogers and Hammerstein proclaimed it to be. It's going on right now, so why don't you pay it a visit?

And give Big Tex my regards.

Of time, telephones, eternity, and Mrs. Appleton

It seems like everybody I see driving a car nowadays is talking on a cell phone.

Now, this certainly isn't news to you. And before you wander over to another section of the paper let me assure you that this isn't going to be an admonition about the safety of driving and using the phone at the same time. I'll leave that battle to someone who can come up with a better argument than I can.

It's just that I see this cell phone epidemic running rampant everywhere. In restaurants. In movie theaters. Even on the way into church, folks get a last little communication fix that will have to last a whole hour.

At the high school where I teach, students are allowed to use their cell phones after the last bell of the day. And, let me tell you, when that bell rings the hallway is like one of those ninja movies where all the warriors whip out their hidden weapons on some secret command.

I sometimes wonder what those kids, and all those cell phone chatterers everywhere else, would do if technology was magically transported back in time about forty or so years.

In Oakwood, the little piney woods town where I grew up, every house had one telephone. At least every house that I went into. And I wandered pretty freely.

That one phone per household was a bulky thing as ugly as a

mud clod and as heavy as a boat anchor. And, for some unexplainable reason, it was always located in the most inconvenient part of the house. Ours sat in a curved wall niche in a narrow hallway directly under a big attic fan that rattled like a freight train when it was on. And it was on all summer. There was no room in there for a chair, so we had to stand up to yell into that phone.

It had no dial, just a glossy smooth front, and you had to crank a little handle on its side to engage it. Then you lifted the heavy handset and told Mrs. Appleton, the operator, who you wanted to talk to. Say, I'd ask to speak to my friend Chris Stevens and Mrs. Appleton would connect us or she'd tell me that the Stevens had gone into Palestine for the afternoon to see a picture show and buy some groceries.

Everybody kept Mrs. Appleton updated as to their whereabouts. She called everyone "honey," and she was a great fount of information.

Sometimes too much.

One time my mother, who had come to our little town from a much larger one that had dial telephones, had asked for some lady who lived out near the Nineveh community because she'd heard that she had a sewing machine for sale.

The Nineveh woman's husband was a butter and egg man, the rural equivalent of a milkman, and Mrs. Appleton told my mother "you don't buy your butter and eggs from them, honey." Then she'd reminded my mother who she *did* use.

It made my mother so angry that she didn't call anybody for the better part of a week. After all, she told us at the supper table, Mrs. Appleton didn't have absolute power and certainly not when it came to where we got our eggs.

I liked Mrs. Appleton and so did everyone else in town. Even my mother, except for that one week.

Anyway, I have to wonder what this current cell phone society would make of one phone in the middle of the house with a human being on the other end of the line who had to direct the call.

I even dreamed about it once. I was at the pearly gates and, instead of Saint Peter, there was just that old black telephone on top of a short marble column. When I picked up the handset a familiar voice asked me where I wanted to go.

And I had to smile, in that dream, since it turned out that Mrs. Appleton ended up having considerably more clout than my mother ever suspected.

One cold October night under a starry sky

Almost a year ago, on the forty-fifth anniversary of the premiere of *The Alamo*, I watched the movie again for the umpteenth time. But this time in the place where it was filmed, within the adobe walls of the movie set John Wayne and Happy Shahan, a south Texas rancher, built on Happy's land near Brackettville.

Karen and I met our friends Dean and Debby Smith out there; Dean had appeared in the movie and in nine more Wayne flicks as stuntman or actor or both. The night before the screening, we all were the guests of Happy Shahan's daughter for dinner at her ranch. Duke Wayne's youngest child, Marisa, was there, and one of his oldest grandchildren, Anita, along with her father Don Lacava, who had been Duke's assistant director on *The Alamo*. All had flown in for the weekend from Los Angeles.

Over good wine and good food, I told Wayne's daughter and granddaughter—the latter being older than the former—a story passed on to me by a lady I'd met recently when I'd given a speech in Alvin. This lady told me she had, one day in the mid-sixties, happened upon a crowd gathered around Wayne at Hobby Airport. He was in Houston to promote *Hellfighters* and was graciously signing autographs and flashing that wide grin of his. When he asked if the big brood of kids with the lady was all hers, she explained that some of them belonged to her best friend, who had had surgery that day at Hermann Hospital.

Wayne whispered something to one of the men with him and swaggered off.

The lady in Alvin told me that the other man got some information from her and the next morning an enormous bouquet of flowers was delivered to her friend's hospital room. The card said *"Get well soon, and get back to those kids. John Wayne."*

The lady had smiled when she told it. Marisa and Anita smiled when they heard it.

"He loved kids," Marisa said. "He'd rather have been in a room full of kids than adults."

Anita swirled some wine around in her glass and took a sip.

"We hear stories like that all the time," she said.

The next night, we all watched *The Alamo* on a big, inflated screen under a late October sky brimming with stars. They played the overture before the film, like they used to do in the old days, when the feature was big and important enough to warrant an overture and an intermission.

Modern audiences who catch the movie on late night television and don't get to hear that overture are cheated out of some of the total effect that Duke Wayne wanted to achieve. *The Alamo* was his baby start to finish. He fought studios, bankers, and a couple of wives to make it, and he hired one of the best composers in the business, Dimitri Tiomkin, to write the score.

That night in Brackettville the sun dropped slowly behind the rugged horizon, the adobe walls fell into shadows and then into darkness, and a bracing chill set in. The audience of several hundred shivered in their jackets or blankets, settling in for the siege. The overture began in total darkness.

It's a haunting piece of music, starting with a galloping refrain that conjures up soldiers and horses and action. Then, unexpectedly, the tone changes completely and a lilting melody floats up like butterflies out of spring clover. Telling us, I believe, even before the first frame of the picture rolls, that this won't all be courage and sacrifice and dying. That it will be about living, too. Joyous, unrepentant *living*.

There's a great line in the movie, when Richard Widmark—as Jim Bowie—tries to convey to Davy Crockett his admiration for Mexico and her people. "They're not afraid to die," he tells him. "But what's more important, they're not afraid to live."

John Wayne didn't write the line. He didn't even deliver it. But it's always his voice I hear when I think of those words, and it's always his life that comes to mind.

Because his was obviously a life that he wasn't afraid to live. And share. Not only with his friends and family, but with total strangers.

Like that lady from Alvin.

And now,
if you please,
a wild goose chase

In one of his stories, O. Henry pens this fine line: "When wild geese honk high of nights, and women with sealskin coats grow kind to their husbands . . . you may know that winter is near at hand."

The sealskin coats bit has always puzzled me. I guess he's saying that those women are, now that cold weather is on the way, looking to upgrade to fur. But the business about those geese is clear as a bell. And pure manna to a reader as fascinated with geese and their seasonal travels as I am.

Geese have made as many appearances in the world's literature as just about any other animal, and more than most. James Fenimore Cooper's character Natty Bumppo kills thousands of them in *The Leatherstocking Tales,* as do James Michener's bay men in *Chesapeake.* And Dickens plops many a fat goose on many a table in his Victorian novels, not the least of which is the giant goose that Scrooge purchases for the Cratchit clan in *A Christmas Carol.*

But my obsession with geese has nothing to do with killing or eating them. I just like to watch for them, and listen for them.

This time of the year, it doesn't get much better on my daily predawn walk than to hear a single, faraway honk. I usually stop walking then, and listen for the reply. Then, if I'm lucky, an abundance of wanderers break into their ancient traveling song. Calling out to each other in the dark sky. Broadcasting, loud and accurately, that change is coming.

My wife Karen and our doctor like to think of my daily walks as being beneficial to my health. But I tend to see them as more useful to my writing since I do a lot of my planning there.

And to my soul since the geese sometimes sing to me.

O. Henry spent some time about a hundred years ago in Houston. But I doubt he was thinking about the Texas Gulf Coast when that sentence came to mind. Though he worked for the *Houston Post*, it seems he was more into embezzlement and doing jail time for it when he was down here. It wasn't until he settled in New York City that he became perhaps the best short story writer ever.

In New York, he would have seen and heard and smelled and felt the magic of autumn every year. And a big part of that magic would have been long formations of geese gliding overhead.

Down here, where Currier and Ives wouldn't have found much to use in their illustrations on most fall days, we have to employ considerable imagination to envision a crisp, golden scenario.

That's why travel agents book so many folks from hereabouts on foliage tours in New England. Because we feel cheated by the usual absence of the season that is supposed to come between summer and winter.

I think that's why we're so happy when the geese make their first appearance, whether stopping over in rice fields and marshes or just sailing on by, keeping to their precise migratory timetable.

Geese can call us to other places. When they start singing high overhead we can close our eyes and envision hills and valleys covered with trees ablaze with splashes of brown and gold and yellow. And red barns beside babbling brooks. And bracing cold air carrying scents of pumpkin.

Even if, when we open our eyes, what we really have is a landscape flat as a tabletop and a humid morning full of mosquitoes.

But geese aren't just reminders; they're sometimes heralds. Often they're harbingers of a strong cold front that nudges them ahead of it. Of a fine blue norther that will send us scurrying toward fireplaces. So, when I hear the geese, I hope for a blustery night, with a cold wind pushing against my window, and a good book beside a crackling fire with Karen.

When I have those things my life somehow makes perfect sense.

The geese are due about now. Those ancient, graceful reminders that the year is making its slow progress toward its conclusion. That nature's laws and customs are in place.

I hope your autumn is a good one. And that the geese sing to you.

Something wonderful

One night in 1958 my Aunt Georgia, in a kindhearted attempt to get our minds off the fact that our mother was in yet another hospital, treated my sister and me to a night at the movies. We saw *South Pacific* in one of those huge downtown theatres that used to exist. The lights went down, the heavy crimson curtain went slowly up, and the overture swelled. Technicolor spilled out into the big room and I fell head over heels in love with Mitzi Gaynor. I was six.

Nearly a half century later, I'm still a little in love with her and still enjoy watching her jog with the other nurses at the edge of the surf under tall, swaying palms, splashing along with all that Arkansas cockeyed optimism radiating.

But I know now that it was more than Miss Gaynor that caught my attention. That night I got my first taste of the genius of Richard Rodgers and Oscar Hammerstein.

Over the next good many years I caught the film versions of their musicals on the late movie, bought the soundtracks on LPs, then eight-track tapes, then cassettes, then CDs and hummed the tunes as I soldiered on through the daily business of living. Finally, I sprung for an expensive—for a high school teacher and coach—seat in the seventh row of the old Music Hall in Houston to see Yul Brynner in his final revival of his signature role in *The King and I*. Lung cancer had taken its very obvious toll and much was made in the press about whether or not he was really up to all that bounding and bellowing. In fact, he would die not too many months later.

But that night he was still very much the King. And when he stepped up to Miss Anna, placed one big hand on her side and lifted the other one high overhead, the entire audience leaned forward just a bit and held its collective breath. Then when he and Anna swirled around in wide circles on that old stage, "Shall We Dance" floating up from the pit, there was magic in that place. Purely and simply.

I've experienced the magic again and again over the years every time I hear a tune by Rodgers and Hammerstein. And every time I think of one of their stories.

As a writer and a teacher of writing, I admire the intricate crafting of a good story, one of the most ancient of human skills. And it's slowly dawned on me, after reading, studying, and teaching the "giants"—Shakespeare and company—that some of the very best yarn spinning of modern times came from a couple of men whose work has rattled pleasantly around in my head for most of my life.

Leaving the sheer magnificence of their music aside—their waltzes alone would be sufficient to keep one humming to the grave—consider the plots themselves.

Moral dilemmas abound. The Nazi youth in *The Sound of Music* either blows the whistle, literally, on the Van Trapp family, among whom is his sixteen going on seventeen sweetheart, or he doesn't. Billy, the carnival barker in *Carousel*, will either be a good husband and father or he won't. The King, after all that waltzing, will either be the man that Anna knows he can be or he won't.

And, in *South Pacific*, its authors chose not to shy away from the issue of racial prejudice as most of the rest of the industry— and the nation—had, but to take it on headfirst. "They Have to be Taught," Lieutenant Cable's lament, is as strong an indict-ment of hatred and injustice as anything produced in those unfortunate days, and it is thought to have been the determining factor in awarding Rodgers and Hammerstein the Pulitzer Prize for the play.

They deserved it. Few writers, of any genre or era or medium, have as effectively mapped the wide sweep of the human experi-ence as well.

I know. I know. Many folks think the musicals and their songs are hopelessly dated. That they are corny as "Kansas in August." That the endings are tied up too conveniently. That real people don't burst into song to the accompaniment of a full orchestra whenever they feel joyous.

But wouldn't it be nice if, occasionally, they did?

Wouldn't that, as one of the King's wives sings to Miss Anna in *The King and I*, be something wonderful?

The curious affair
of the
reappearing books

When the fellow who was destined to be my father got home from World War II, one of first things that caught his attention was the young widow who ran a bookshop in the front room of her parents' big house in Livingston.

So he bought a book (that he never read), married her and moved her and her six year old daughter and all of the unsold books a hundred or so miles northwest to the little town where he would resume his duties as superintendent of schools.

Oakwood didn't have a bookstore nor much need for one. The people there either did not read much—other than the Dallas or Palestine newspapers, *Life* magazine or *Grit*—or they made do with whatever offering clattered into their mailboxes from the Book-of-the-Month Club or the Literary Guild.

So my mother's books went into closed cabinets in the utility room. Where, some years after I made my entrance, I found them.

I would sit cross-legged on top of the big deep freezer, the tall cabinet doors all open so I could read the titles of those books. Most, of course, held little interest for a boy of nine or ten or whatever I was. But some did. Some promised adventure. Like *Starling of the White House*, that some of you—the ones who pay attention—might remember was the subject of this business some weeks ago.

Most of the volumes were wartime issues, so the paper was inferior, and by the time I came along to inspect them, they had mellowed into a brittle, pie crust brown. Some of the back covers bore not a photograph of the author, but an encouragement to buy war bonds. The first novel I ever read was one that I pulled down from that cabinet. It was *The Yellow Room*, a mystery by Mary Roberts Rinehart. That was followed by a few more and, all of a sudden, I was a reader. But a reader of books that had been out of circulation for a couple of decades. There were some Faulkners and Steinbecks and Hemingways, but not too many. She had actually managed to sell those, I suspect, before closing up shop. Mostly they were works by people you've never heard of.

I moved on to books from the little library in our school, to *King Solomon's Mines* and Sherlock Holmes's adventures. My mother's books stayed behind their closed doors. I grew up. She died. My father sold the house in Oakwood and moved away. Then he died.

Many years later, when I had taught literature for longer than my high school students had been alive, those books came back again.

My brother-in-law undertook to refurbish a small cabin on his family farm so the family could congregate there in the piney woods, and Karen and I could go there on weekends and watch birds and write, respectively. As he was tearing the little place apart, in order to put it back together, he discovered deep in the back of a dark and moldy cabinet, several old cardboard boxes of—you guessed it. Some water had gotten into them, so a few are stained at the edges.

How they got there is anybody's guess. They were quickly stashed away, I imagine, when my father sold the Oakwood house. None of us could have done the easy thing and thrown them away. Because they were books. And because they had belonged to someone we all loved and missed.

So my two sisters and I divided them up. This collection of titles that would have been found in any bookshop in any American town during the early 1940s. None of them are important volumes that bibliophiles will appreciate being saved.

But, to me, they are pretty near priceless.

Because when I read them, I try not to see the stories—usually dated and sometimes downright trite—through the eyes of someone who writes and teaches. But I imagine my mother, long gone, reading them first, when their pages were crisp and their covers sharp. She would always read with a pencil close at hand. And little notes in her wobbly hen-scratching sometimes appear in the margins. Like treasures that have floated down the years.

I put a few of her books on my bookshelves. Others, I've boxed up and stored away. But I know better than to try to get rid of them.

Like the phoenix rising from the ashes, they'll just come back again.

All I know is what I read in the newspaper

If you happen to be reading this in the paper, as opposed to reading it on a computer monitor, then you might be interested to know that you are participating in a hands-on activity that has been around since some time in the 1500s.

That's when, according to my exhaustive research—which means I Googled it—the first newspaper came off the first press somewhere over in Europe. And when, almost certainly, somebody found something in it to write a letter to the editor about.

I don't know about you, but I love reading the paper. In fact, my first voyage each day is out into the dark front yard to pick up the two that we subscribe to. Then, while the coffee is brewing, I take out the sections that don't interest me. I have no head for business or finance (my literary agent and my banker will concur here) so those sections get yanked. The classified ads are the next to go, except on Saturday, when I want to see if there are any garage sales on my walking route. I walk later than usual on Saturdays, after the sun comes up, and I carry a few dollars in my pocket in case I pass a sale with any used books.

On Sundays, taking out the sections of the two papers is a real chore, sort of like field-dressing a deer. With all the advertisements and flyers, not to mention the fat real estate and automobile and employment sections (I have the house, the car, and the job that I'll have to make do with for a while), I end up tossing more than I keep.

But what I *do* keep is the perfect way to start every day.

Early mornings at our house find Karen propped up in bed with our tribe—Will and Grace and Missy and Earl Gray—in close attendance. Yours truly is in an overstuffed chair on the other side of the bedroom. We both have big mugs of hot coffee, a reporter chatters away on the TV, newspaper pages and cats are spread out all over the place, and bliss abides.

Those papers are my daily reminders that the world is still spinning out there in the darkness. First, I read the local obituaries. Not, as George Burns used to say, to see if I am in them, but to see who else is. Then I flip over to the opinion pages, just to see who's mad about what. Next up is a visit with a columnist or two.

Then I scan the headlines—avoiding some of the stories completely, dipping in for a quick look-see in a few, reading others from start to finish. I conclude with my favorite comic strips. It's not so much saving the best for last: it's more like having dessert.

Ever since I first picked up reading as a skill and a habit, I've picked up the daily paper to check in with the world.

And there's just not much better than to come across an old, *old* paper. Say, from sixty or more years ago. Those publications—even the ads—are wonderful mirrors of their eras. Of who those people were. Of what they bought and how much it cost. Even a cursory look proves that they had to put up with war and moral decline and corruption in government. Just like we do.

It's all there, in black and white. As fine and accurate a history as you are likely to find.

People ask me sometimes if I ever read the paper on the computer or any of the new online novels. And I always say no.

I would no sooner read a novel on a computer screen than I would eat a gourmet dinner in my car at a drive in. Because there is more to enjoying good food than just shoveling it down. There is the ambiance of the setting and the pleasure of the company of other diners.

And there is more to reading a book or a newspaper than simply processing the words. There's the crinkle of the big pages and the smell of the newsprint, and the texture of the binding and the spine. There's the thing itself—tangible and solid—that I can put down and then take up again. Or just hold for a moment while I mull over a passage or a fact.

Someday, I suppose, if society keeps up its march toward pure technology, newspapers and books will be gone completely.

But by then, hopefully, so will I. For I wouldn't find the world nearly as interesting without them.

At Thanksgiving

When you gather with your family this Thursday, I'll wager that more than a few of you will be thinking, much of the time, of other Thursdays.

This will depend on your age, of course, and on the number of Thanksgivings that you have enjoyed. Or survived. That distinction depending largely on the people with whom you gather. If they are difficult folk—overbearing, blunt, ill-mannered; the list of possibilities is a long one and you could probably add to it—then the day is likely to be something you'll just want to be done with. And then promptly forget.

I've logged fifty-four Turkey Days, myself. And, though I can't attest to the nature of the first few, I can happily report that this particular holiday accounts for some of my fondest memories.

Thanksgivings in Oakwood, my East Texas hometown, were outstanding when I was a boy. Especially if a big blustery norther had blown in, scattering oak and sycamore leaves, some as big as saucers, all over the place. When everything was brown and yellow, the sky was slate-gray, when one of my father's carefully laid fires roared and popped in the fireplace, and the aroma of my mother's roasted turkey and fresh-baked pecan and sweet potato pies drifted through the whole house. When family members would come in and chatter and hug everybody and we'd all try to imagine what the floats in the Macy's parade on the television would look like in color.

That's how I remember all of those early Thanksgivings. But, of course, memory is sometimes a liar, and some of them were surely sad or rainy or downright hot. But I've erased those and what I have left were all Norman Rockwell affairs.

I do recall that the 1963 meeting was a little somber. My sister's husband had died in a car accident in May. Then President Kennedy was assassinated a few days before Thanksgiving. But Walter Cronkite said on the television that we should, as Americans, make the best of the situation and count our blessings. So we did. We generally paid attention to Walter Cronkite.

A decade later found me in the army, stationed in a small town in Bavaria. Thanksgiving is not a German holiday, of course, so the cooks at our mess hall went all out to provide a festive occasion. There were fat turkeys and all the trimmings, pies—mincemeat and pumpkin and fruit—and even wine on every table. We were all turned out in our class A uniforms and were on our best behavior. The soldiers' wives and children came on base for that repast and even some of the Germans from that little village, Illesheim. The base commander, a colonel who always wore a big pistol on his side, didn't wear it that day. He made a toast; one of the chaplains said a prayer. Then we all tucked into one of the finest meals I've ever had. I still have the little printed menu somewhere.

The following year I had mustered out and got myself back into college, and an army buddy from northern Arkansas, who had been in my platoon in Germany, drove down to Oakwood to share Thanksgiving with my dad, my sisters, and me. My mother had died in January, so it was something of a sad occasion. But my friend being there was a blessing. As was the Cowboys-Redskins game that afternoon. When an untested backup quarterback named Clint Longley came in for the injured Roger

Staubach and stood flat-footed and threw the football pretty much the length of the field to win the game.

As time went by, and the years stacked up, Thanksgivings became as much cradles of memories as current events.

Nowadays, when I sit down for that big dinner, I always sense the presence of more people than are actually there. Like my parents, grandparents, uncles and aunts. And good friends that have gone on.

And I'll bet that's the way it is with your gathering, too.

So, this Thursday, when you sit down to eat more than you should, take a good, long look around the table and be thankful—to whomever or whatever you choose to be thankful—for all the people there. Even the ones that exist only in your memory.

Because memory, I've come to realize, is one of the richest blessings of all. Even if it lies occasionally.

You have a wonderful Thanksgiving. And eat a second piece of pie.

Walking, strutting, marching and John Wayne

Have you ever considered how one little word can ignite a search for a whole slew of better ones?

Take "walk" for example.

Amble is a better word than walk. So is strut. And meander. "Walk" is too generic. It's like that drawer in your kitchen where everything ends up; it's a utility player, the general practitioner of words meaning to put one foot in front of the other. Amble and strut and meander are specialists. So are totter and march and stroll and stagger and saunter.

Walking is what somebody you can't bring clearly into focus does. It is just movement with no regard to character or detail. Ambling, on the other hand, is what your fifth-grade teacher used to do when she moved down the rows to watch her students work. She took her time. She strolled. And strutting is what that prissy girl that works at the diner does. The one who pops her gum while she struts out with your blue plate special. She infuses even that simple range of movement with an attitude. She prances.

When that fifth-grade teacher told you to march yourself right down to the principal's office, you knew what she meant. She didn't say to meander, and she certainly didn't say to strut, which would mean that you would have to do it with an attitude, which was probably the very thing that got you into hot water in the first place.

She wouldn't have said to run or rush down there, because that would imply that it might be a pleasant journey, that you might actually enjoy the trip. What she wanted was for you to move in a direct and straightforward manner. No nonsense (a good word). No shenanigans (a better one). March! She knew precisely what she wanted. And so did you.

There are plenty of better words than walk precisely because there are plenty of different types of walking.

Let's use John Wayne as proof positive of that. If you've been visiting this little corner of the paper for any length of time and haven't figured out by now that John Wayne ranks pretty high on my list of essentials, then you just haven't been paying attention.

Sometimes John Wayne floated as much as he walked. Wobbling off course like a gyroscope gone berserk. Ambling. His big arm pushing forward like a swimmer caught in a strong current. His legs taking almost impossibly tiny steps. Sometimes he was like a dust devil, like a sudden whirlwind drifting along in a field, tilting this way and that, finally playing itself out. The major difference being that when he stopped he might just wallop somebody.

Watch him swagger off toward the little cottage where Maureen O'Hara is waiting for him in *The Quiet Man*, listing so far to port that it seems, for just an instant, that he might lose his balance altogether, crashing heavily into the earth like a felled oak.

He doesn't, of course. Falling isn't any more of a possibility than flying. Then sometimes he moves so resolutely forward that there's no swagger at all. No ambling. Watch him eat up the ground in the climactic scene in *Red River*, like a locomotive in full steam, dead set on making short work of Montgomery Clift when he gets to him. Now watch him move, exhausted, down the gangplank in an early scene of *In Harm's Way*. He's slouching along now, nearly used up. His warship looms gray and massive behind him in the dark night, in port to be knocked back together after a fight, welders' sparks exploding in little bursts along her side. His arm is in a sling; his brow is low over weary eyes that are no more than slits. He's beat up, like his ship. But both of them are still here, needing just a little rest before hitting another lick.

Watch him cross the cabin's threshold from darkness into light in *The Searchers*. He's darn near limping now, out into a new day. Out into yet another screwed-up situation that he'll have to fix.

There were as many variations of John Wayne's walk as there were situations the characters he played found themselves in. And—guess what?—the same is true for you and the situations you find yourself in.

Thus endeth the lesson on the action verb "walk" and its proxies. Your assignment is to, when tempted to use that word, pick yourself a better one. Because specificity is one of the things that separates interesting people from boring ones, and true wordsmiths from lazy communicators. There's just too many of those.

I'll amble on now. You have a nice stroll over into December.

Oh, we fools
that fool with
Mother Nature

On the day after Thanksgiving, Karen and I drove our daughter Kara to the Dallas airport from my sister's house in McKinney, where we had all overstuffed ourselves nicely with food and fellowship. After we dropped her off at her gate in the early morning, we found ourselves some coffee and charted our way across Dallas to Interstate 45 and our journey home.

Karen had the map and I told her I'd drive anywhere she told me to as long as it didn't involve getting close to any shopping malls. It was Black Friday, remember, and I'd watched the clogged traffic and fanatical shoppers on my sister's television before we left.

So, we avoided the freeways—malls generally live close to freeways—and took old Loop 12 that, though long ago relegated to minor loop status by bigger satellites, still meanders its way along the outskirts of the city through old neighborhoods full of old houses under old trees. It was early enough for some morning fog to have lingered, and for us to pretty much have the road to ourselves.

The trees along that drive were absolutely beautiful in their autumn attire. For a stretch of twenty miles or more, right there on the periphery of one heck of a big, sprawling city, we could have been on one of those foliage tours in New England that people shell out big bucks for.

Of course, we had to look up at the trees themselves, carefully avoiding anything manmade that was beneath them. Like the rundown houses with bars on their windows. And the rough-looking stores in the shabby neighborhoods. And the graffiti on overpasses and what was left of any wooden fences that hadn't fallen down or been replaced by chain-link.

Those glorious trees, multicolored and majestic, rose up above garbage and clutter and exhaust fumes, sending their leaves floating down into places that didn't look deserving of them. It all served to confirm my long-held belief that Nature just pretty much puts up with us.

I may be wrong about this, of course. You could line up any ten people you can find and it's a pretty safe bet that at least six of them would know more about science than I do.

But I'm pretty sure that the earth doesn't really need us at all. We scar it up, cement it over, plunder its bounties, and deplete its resources, and it keeps on at its work. In spite of us.

I'll bet that if civilization vanished completely, like it does occasionally in my creative writing students' stories, then forests and fields would just grow over the foolishness that we left behind and, pretty soon, there wouldn't be much left to prove that we'd been here at all.

But, of course, we keep hacking away under the banner of progress. When a business goes belly-up, we leave the building there as some sort of monument to the owner's misfortune or folly. Then, when a new business cranks up, no thought is given to using an existing structure, so a new building appears. If I ever get to be king, I intend to outlaw such behavior, and decree that when somebody abandons a place, they have to remove it completely. Then nature can rightfully reclaim what was hers to begin with.

Until I see staggeringly convincing evidence to the contrary, I'll go on believing that the earth, in her ancient, boundless wisdom, will survive anything we come up with. Those stately, determined trees at the edge of Dallas reminded me of that.

I'll let one of my favorite poets, Carl Sandburg, have the last words on the matter. He penned these lines eighty or so years ago about how the earth heals the scars left by mankind's activities:

Pile the bodies high at Austerlitz and Waterloo.
Shovel them under and let me work –
I am the grass; I cover all.
And pile them high at Gettysburg
And pile them high at Ypres and Verdun.
Shovel them under and let me work.
Two years, ten years, and passengers ask the conductor:
What place is this?
Where are we now?
I am the grass.

Let me work.

Two ghosts of
Christmas past
fallen on hard times

We come now to the matter of fruitcakes and mincemeat pies. Delicacies that are, in my family, totally unappreciated by everyone but yours truly.

Therefore, my chances of having a serving of either of them this holiday season are somewhere up there with the Houston Texans going to the Super Bowl in January.

Be that as it may, I still am in favor of this pair of seasonal delights that, for whatever reason, seem to have slipped almost completely out of favor nowadays. I ran them through my stellar research team—Google.com—and learned a little about their histories.

The origin of the fruitcake was in ancient Rome and, ironically, didn't involve fruit at all. Honey, pomegranate seeds, pine nuts, and raisins were stirred into barley mash and baked. Mincemeat, as you probably already know and as some of you more seasoned readers might remember, was originally made with real meat, a not too tantalizing bit of business called suet. But way before even that, in Elizabethan England, mince pies were born of the need to preserve meat whose freshness was getting a bit iffy by soaking it in brandy and hiding it in fruit and nuts in a pastry. Both recipes have changed considerably, a fact for which those of us who fancy them can be thankful.

In Truman Capote's fine memoir A Christmas Memory, his eccentric old relative announced one cold morning during the Great Depression that "it's fruitcake weather!" Whereupon she and young Truman went about locating the necessary ingredients: flour, eggs, candied fruit, sugar, raisins, spices, nuts, and whiskey. The old lady was of the opinion that any fruitcake worth anything had to have a generous splash of whiskey stirred into the batter and another one drizzled over the whole thing when it came out of the oven. Which sounds like a good plan to me.

I don't remember if my mother ever actually made a fruitcake, but we always got several in the mail when I was a boy in East Texas. My father, being the superintendent of schools, got lots of stuff from textbook and school supply and sporting goods salesmen, and fruitcakes were common gifts in those days. Those cakes came from Eilenberger's in Palestine or from the famous Collins Street Bakery in Corsicana.

A good many years later, my wife Karen and our daughters turned up their noses at one of those Collins Street masterpieces that I'd ordered. They sniffed it and eyed it from every angle and you'd have thought I'd slapped a haggis or a hog's head cheese on the table.

I told them that I'd read that famous folk like Danny Thomas, Gregory Peck, Frank Sinatra, and Judy Garland had been fans of the Collins Street cakes. But my logic was faulty, as my logic quite often tends to be. Since our daughters didn't know who any of those people were, they weren't likely to be sufficiently impressed to eat even one morsel of something they considered gross.

Then Karen chimed in, if I recall correctly, with the fact that all of those people were dead. Which didn't help my case.

So I had to conclude that my fruitcake eating days were over.

Needless to say, I had no better luck with mincemeat pie; though I do score a good slab of that at Luby's occasionally.

Realistically, one glance at the numbers on the bathroom scales—not to mention a closet full of old clothes that I can sometimes hear laughing at me—should be ample proof that I ought to steer clear of cake and pie of any sort.

But I do love the nutty-sweet, spicy flavors of these two old friends who have hit the skids. They taste like Christmas to me. They taste of Dickens and holly and winter. And a slice of one or the other—or both—by the fireplace with a hot cup of coffee is fine, indeed.

So, now that we're in the final run-up to the holidays, in the unlikely event that you're offered a slice of fruitcake or mincemeat pie, either accept it graciously or, if you don't care for it, at least don't frown. Or laugh out loud. Show a little respect for two old traditions that have long, proud pedigrees.

Not to mention a handful of persistent and devoted fans.

The chilling confessions
of a
weather junkie

As I write this, a monster norther is tumbling its way down the continent from the arctic. Of course, by the time you read it, it may very well be eighty degrees outside.

But right now it is early in the morning, way before daylight, on the last day of November. The other living things in this house—one wife and four cats—are fast asleep and the only sounds in the place are the tapping I'm doing on the keyboard of my laptop and the ticking of the little clock on the desk in my study.

Outside my windows it is dark and humid and still. And that big cold front is making its way toward all of us—house and wife and cats and yours truly—as surely as a fast train on a beeline for a depot.

I'm a weather junkie. I'll confess that right up front. There's not much more impressive and beautiful, to me, than a wide, gunmetal gray sky full of a dark and brooding thunderstorm. The low clouds so full of their cargo that it seems impossible that they can stay aloft. The air rich with the heady promise of rain.

And a windy day—a real Winnie-the-Pooh blustery day— calls me out into it every time. A day when trees dance briskly in a stiff headwind and fields of tall grass roll and sway like the choppy surface of an agitated lake. A day like that is perfection personified. It is, as C. S. Lewis might have said, red meat and strong beer.

This fascination with meteorological events has worked its way into all of my books. My memoir about my father and his Alzheimer's experience commences in Oakwood, the little town we lived in, covered in snow one Christmas Eve a long time ago. Then I set an historical novel in the Galveston hurricane of 1900. Three books later—each of them sprinkled liberally with rain, wind, or snow—I started my latest yarn with a little boy waiting for the first blue norther of the season with his old grandfather during World War II. The two of them go out into the yard to meet it, reach up and touch it, and even imagine they can smell what it brings with it: scents of pine and fir from the Dakotas, and sweet corn and musty wheat from Kansas.

I called that novel *Touching Winter*. And that's what I intend to do later this morning, when that big fellow finally gets here.

It hit Dallas late yesterday afternoon, and my sister Janie sat on her patio and gave me a play-by-play account of its arrival over her cell phone: the dark sky, her wind chimes playing a lively tune and leaves scurrying. Then the sudden plunge into the deep freezer. Finally she was quiet for a moment, before summing the whole experience up with a pair of soft words: "It's amazing."

Now, some people might conclude that my sister is as crazy as I am. But I like to think that we're—along with my wife, who is also a weather junkie—just a little better off than people who can't manage to see turbulent weather as anything more than an inconvenience.

I intend to go outside later this morning and put the palm of my hand right up against that arctic freight train as it arrives. I'll take my Creative Writing III class out there with me if it happens during our time together. Because I couldn't come up with a better lesson for people wanting to be writers than to put them in the presence of something bigger than all of us. Something so compelling that, try as mankind might, we can't stop it. Or even slow it down. All we can do when facing something like that is either get out of its way or stand in awe of it.

Everything comes at a cost, of course, and society can fall out of balance as quickly as nature does. Lots of unfortunate folks will have to scramble for shelter tonight. And my heart goes out to them.

But, this early morning, as November slips into December, and as a strong norther bears heavily down, I'm looking forward to its arrival. To its looming appearance on the northern horizon as it announces, with confident authority, that things will change now.

It's comforting to know—in a world that is usually altogether too confusing and hectic—that there are some things that I'm not expected to have any control over whatsoever. That's probably why I love the weather so much.

Today's paper just plopped into the yard outside my windows. Earl Gray the cat has appeared, yawning, by my chair. A hundred or so miles to the north, a massive giant is galloping in this direction.

And I can't wait.

Christmas Eve

Much of the world stands vigil today and tonight.

Countless millions are waiting for the anniversary of what Christians believe to have been the turning point in the totality of human experience: a humble event in a mean place in a far-away land two millennia ago that provided the resounding crack that has rung through all of history.

Now, whatever you happen to believe or not believe in regards to that lofty ideology doesn't alter the fact that Christmas Eve tends to be a day built for waiting. For family to arrive. For airplanes to land. For food to come out of the oven. For stores to close so that all the buying can finally screech to a halt.

It just seems that everybody—no matter what their race, age, religion or lack thereof—is waiting for something on this long winter night. For something better that might arrive with the sunrise.

It's a day brimming with tradition and memories for me. I grew up in a family that put great stock in Christmas and in a house that did it justice. That old wood-framed structure in a little East Texas town fairly burst with holiday spirit. From my mother's various treats—pecan-crusted cheese logs and sweet potato pies and divinity—to my father's last minute shopping in Miss Tine Lambert's five and dime and the ritualistic splitting of the annual coconut. Coconuts were strange and exotic items in that place and time, and my father always managed to work the bashing of one into the Christmas festivities.

Late in the afternoon, I'd help him haul in firewood for the stack he kept on the front porch, then I'd watch my mother wrap the last of the gifts on top of a big deep-freezer in the utility room, both of us watching darkness descend outside, as if real magic was at work.

My parents have been gone for a long time and, every Christmas Eve, I light a pair of candles for them on a little table by a window in our entryway. I've watched, from the front yard, the flickering lights of candles in that window for lots of years now. And in all weathers: cold, hot, rainy, and even in a New England-worthy snowfall a couple of years ago. I like to think that my mother and father watch them too, from wherever they are. I like to think that they are particularly close by on this night that still holds considerable magic as I wait.

Tonight, whatever you believe or choose not to believe, I hope you'll be standing vigil, also. Waiting for an end to war and meanness and suffering and hunger. Waiting for peace. A permanent peace that will engulf the world like a warm blanket.

It might not happen, I realize. Odds are it won't. But what's the harm in waiting for it? And hoping?

Dylan Thomas—that tortured poet who located perfection in words but not in life and finally drank himself to death—wrote a little book about a holiday from his boyhood, surely one of his only happy memories. He ends A Child's Christmas in Wales with these now famous sentences:

> *Looking through my bedroom window, out into the moonlight and the unending smoke-colored snow, I could see the lights in the windows of all the other houses on our hill and hear the music rising from them up the long, steadily falling night. I turned the gas down, I got into bed.*

I said some words to the close and holy darkness, and then
I slept.

Tonight, Karen and I will serve our traditional Christmas Eve chili and cornbread to our family. We'll all laugh through good memories and watch our quartet of cats slap at decorations on the tree that they assume was put there for them. Then I'll go out-side, look at my house, and watch the pinpoints of light dance on my parents' candles, certain that the people inside that house will remember, on some future Christmas Eve, to light one for me.

And for that—and much more—I'll say some words, this night, to the close and holy darkness.

New Year's Eve

Tonight, as one year slips into another one, legions of revelers in unbecoming hats—and perhaps of wobbly balance, dependent upon the amount of reveling having been undertaken —will kiss the person or persons nearest to them, lift their glass aloft, and join in the singing of a song. The meaning of which, most likely, will be completely beyond them.

When most folks sing a couple of stanzas of "Auld Lang Syne," they might as well be singing "Hail to the Chief" or "Yes, We Have no Bananas." No other song that I know of is so universally known by heart and, at the same time, so universally misunderstood.

Somebody once asked me—after a college graduation in which the graduates all held hands and sang the song—what the words meant. And the best answer I could come up with was the one my high school English teacher gave me eons ago: that it sort of means "even though we may never all be in this place together again, part of our hearts will."

The most literal translation of "auld lang syne" seems to be "times gone by." A sentiment that conjures up memory and nostalgia. And it is altogether fitting and proper for us to give voice to such emotions on New Year's Eve, even if we don't understand the phrase we're giving voice to.

We owe this tradition, and this enigma, to Robert Burns, that grand lad of eighteenth-century Scottish poetry who found God and beauty in fields and trees and deep highland lochs. And free drinks wherever he could locate them.

He wrote in a rich Scottish dialect that can pose an almost insurmountable stumbling block for English students. And for their teachers, too, unless they loosen up and choose to have a little fun with it.

This spring, when we get to Mr. Burns in my English IV classes, I intend to rattle off that sing-song enunciation like I know exactly what I'm doing.

Because, when we take up his "To a Mouse," we'll be tackling a poem that hides a deep, abiding truth under the funny-sounding brogue, just as "Auld Lang Syne" does. In "To a Mouse," the poet, while plowing, upends a field mouse out of the underground burrow the rodent had carefully built in which to sleep away the quickly approaching winter. Now the burrow is destroyed and the mouse is doomed.

And Burns, musing over the situation, comes up with a couple of lines that have lived long after both him and the mouse: "The best-laid schemes o' mice an men gang aft agley."

Which, after my students finish laughing at my East Texas butchering of the highland phrasing, they will come to realize hits upon a bittersweet reality. That the best-made plans, of any of us, sometimes fall apart.

So, I'll tell them, it's a good idea to have a back-up plan or two in place. Which, sadly, that mouse did not. Too many kids in school now have pointed themselves in one direction so completely that, should something go amiss, they think they are done for, that all will be lost. Maybe they won't get accepted at the college they want. That's when I tell them there are other colleges open for business. Maybe they won't end up with the boyfriend or girlfriend they've had their eye on since the third grade.

They'll have to face it; that plan "gang aft agley." Time for a new plan.

And one short poem by a long-dead Scottish poet usually gets that point across better than anything else could. "To a Mouse" ends with Burns telling the hopeless little fellow that, in one way, he is better off than his "fellow earth-bound mortal," meaning himself, in that the mouse only lives in the present. Never in the past or the future. So he doesn't have to suffer through bad memories or anxious planning. "But, Och!," the poet says, "I backward cast my eye, on prospects drear! And forward, tho' I canna see, I guess an' fear."

At the end of the day—or, as is the case today, the year—what it comes down to is this: all of us are pretty much just guessing and fearing. Flying by the seats of our pants into long days and nights that are as uncertain as the weather.

So, tonight, when we once again sing Robert Burn's immortal words about—we're pretty sure—times gone by, let's drink that cup of kindness cheer, get a little sleep, and then get on with our guessing and fearing in a brand new year.

I hope it's a good one for you, with few, if any, of your plans gang aft agley.

Quiet, please

Now that the new year has found its feet and is standing upright and taking baby steps toward wherever it's going, I'd like to make a suggestion. Actually, what I'd like to do is issue a request. And it can be encapsulated neatly and succinctly into one word.

Quiet.

I don't know about you, but what I'd like to have in these early days of 2007 is a big dose of pure, blissful quiet. And right now, in what is as close to the dead of winter as we're likely to get with our geography and along our latitude, it seems a perfect time for it.

I'm pretty much fed up with the unrelenting noise that echoes out of shopping malls and football stadiums and packed restaurants and even family gatherings. I'm one of those people who can sit perfectly contented in a room with no sound at all other than the occasional turning of the pages of the book I am reading. Sometimes, to me, the most wonderful sound in creation is not a sound at all, but the total absence of it. Sometimes, in fact, all of the televisions and radios and stereos in the house being turned off is a blessing of the highest order.

Not all the time, mind you. Don't go thinking I'm some sort of nut about this or that I've taken up the banner of anti-technology or am ready for the monastery. Whole cadres of loud commotions make up my life, and I'm generally as happy as a cat napping in the sunshine among them. There are ball games, marching bands, big classes full of students full of sap and ready to spill over with opinions and questions, television shows, talkative friends, and even whole operas full of caterwauling.

But, right now—as the temperature dips and brisk northerly winds whip through—give me good, abiding, joyful quiet. Let me read away the hours by the fireplace or on the patio among a carpet of leaves. Give me a comfortable chair on the porch of the little cabin on a hilltop that we often retreat to up near Elkhart, where the only thing I'm likely to hear is the occasional chatter between two mockingbirds.

In a few months, I'll climb out of this auditory hibernation and be up for the clamor of an Astros game, the cacophony of city streets and children yelling at each other in the yards of our neighborhood. I might even dig out my little portable radio and listen to either the antics of a couple of witty disc jockeys on my predawn morning walk or, if I'm in a more serious mood, to the droll, thoughtful musings of the commentators on National Public Radio. I might listen to some jazz while I take my walk, or something downright rousing. Strauss, maybe; all those tubas and cymbals might be just the thing.

But not yet. For a while yet—in this quiet and ordinary time of the year—I'd much rather just plod along my old, dependable walking trail with nothing more to listen to than my own thoughts taking shape. Or a flock of geese honking high overhead.

Over the holidays, Karen and I took a walk along a quiet suburban street in North Texas. A stiff, cold wind set the bare branches of a row of huge crape myrtle trees to rattling against each other, like drumsticks tapping out the slow, whispered cadence for some ancient ritual.

If it hadn't been so quiet—if cars had been zipping along that street or we'd been yakking at each other or listening to Walkman radios—we would have missed out on that mesmerizing concert being played just for us. And that would have been a significant loss, indeed.

Robert Louis Stevenson—who wrote awfully loud stories full of swashbuckling and pirates and sea battles—maintained that "quiet minds cannot be perplexed or frightened but go on in fortune or misfortune at their own private pace, like a clock during a thunderstorm."

So, one of my New Year's resolutions is to try to be more like the clock than the thunderstorm. For, as Adlai Stevenson once said, "In quiet places, reason abounds."

My mother, a quiet woman, voted for Mr. Stevenson twice for president. My father was quiet, also, but he was an Eisenhower man.

Once upon a time, maybe, in the deep piney woods

When I was doing research for the book that would become *Warden*, I came across a couple of references to one of those yarns that tumbles from generation to generation and stands equal chances of being fact or folklore.

So, come with me now to Huntsville, Texas, in 1848. And remember, I don't offer this as history. Just conjecture.

The morning might have gone something like this.

One of three men carefully stepping off a distance might have stopped, looked again at the wide expanse of hilltop all around him, and thought that it was almost too fine a place for a penitentiary to be built on.

Another of them might have mopped his brow with a hand-kerchief or a bandanna. It was August and it had to have been stifling hot in East Texas.

The three men had been appointed by the governor, and their purpose had been set forth clearly by the first legislature elected after Texas had made its transition from a republic to a state. They were to select a site no larger than one hundred acres that would cost no more than five dollars each. They had finally settled on Huntsville and paid $22.00 for the 4.8 acres they were presently stepping off. The prison itself would be built there. Another 94 acres not too far away, thick with timber, was bought for $470.00.

The legislation had been specific in its requirements. It must be in a healthful climate and near a navigable body of water so that machinery, tools and materials could be brought in, and articles made by the convicts sent out. Rehabilitation held no particular importance in the agenda of that first legislature, but profit most certainly did. The Trinity River was close-by, so those articles—whatever they turned out to be—could be shipped down to Galveston's busy port.

Those three fellows, as they plotted the giant outline, must have tried to envision the "secure wall" that the legislation had mandated, made of "substantial materials" that would enclose a yard large enough for workshops to be constructed. For the convicts were to be kept busy performing whatever officials "deemed most profitable and useful to the state."

It would have to be one heck of a wall, they must have figured.

Several of the citizens of Huntsville must have wandered up the slight hill from town to watch the three at their task. The children would have arrived first, drawn to any activity that promised a respite from their chores. Then some of the men would have come, lumbering and stoic and chewing tobacco. A few of them had fought at San Jacinto just a dozen years before. Some had lost friends or relatives at the Alamo. Most of them had been citizens of the United States, then Mexico, then the Republic of Texas, and now the United States again. But all of that meant little, when weighed against getting in a crop, or cutting timber, or selling enough goods in their stores to provide for their families.

One of the men might have stood apart from the others, leaning on a handsome walking stick that he always carried. He wasn't infirm, or old enough to need a cane, but it did serve to steady him on occasion when he had drunk to excess. And the common consensus was that he did that pretty often.

Now one of the townspeople might have walked over to him. He wasn't sure whether to address him as General, or Congressman, or Mr. President. At present he was a United States Senator, home for the summer recess, but a couple of the handles seemed, to the man, to outweigh that. So he didn't call him anything, but just asked his question.

"Is there any truth to the story," the man from town wanted to know, "that this here was all something in the way of a trade-off? That Austin got the legislature, and we ended up with the prison?"

The other man leaned on his walking stick then, and probed at some pine straw and twigs with the toe of one big boot. He probably thought a moment before he spoke, and maybe watched some of the children who had by that time lost interest in the meager activity of the committee and were chasing each other around.

"I've been involved with a few legislatures in my day," the man with the stick is supposed to have finally answered. He would have smiled then, and very likely he spat.

"And, all in all, I figure we'll come out far ahead with a prison."

It might have happened like that, before that prison—that is still a prison to this day—was built and christened The Walls. Before the man with the stick became a race track and a university and a big statue beside a freeway. When Sam Houston was a real man.

A little gossip
won't hurt you,
unless it's about you

It was President Teddy Roosevelt's daughter Alice who, in her very old age, used to greet guests at her Washington parties with "If you don't have anything nice to say about someone, come sit right here by me."

Alice was something of a handful, by all accounts. I'm an avid reader of just about any book or article I can find about the capital city and its history, and she pops up pretty regularly during virtually any part of the twentieth century, usually as the source of some witty or caustic remark. She was a teenager when her father was president, and when a reporter asked him once about one of her exploits, he famously replied that he could either run the country or he could control Alice; he couldn't do both.

Ms. Roosevelt—young, old and in between—apparently loved a good serving of gossip. And—let's just face it at the outset—many, many people do.

Now, I'm not talking about knowing something that other people do not. Most people love to be the first herald in with a bit of news. Like a pony express rider pulling his steed to a dramatic stop, jumping down into a billowing cloud of dust, and delivering the goods.

That's normal, I imagine. But it's when the sharing of news becomes the distribution of slander—be it true or false—that a true gossip is born.

One of the standard lead-ins employed by most gossips is "I guess you knew that ..." Which are words that they somehow manage to recite with a straight face, in spite of the fact that they actually hope that you *don't* know it.

"I guess you knew that he left his wife." Or "I guess you knew that he filed bankruptcy." Or "I guess you knew that he crossed the picket line."

Now, these things might very well have happened fifty years ago; that's not likely to slow a veteran gossip down. A gossip good at his calling can recall old events as quick as a hiccup. It's a gift, I guess.

Then, after plopping down the bad news like a rump roast on a butcher's block, a good gossip will, to make sure the point has been driven solidly home, conclude with what I call the "closer." A really first-rate gossip will end with "I didn't know if you knew that." As sort of a justification for lowering the boom, to bring you up to speed.

I'm not sure what motivates a gossip other than the obvious satisfaction of knowing something about someone and the enjoyment of blabbing it. Maybe there's a comfortable nirvana—a warm safe-haven—born of the fact that these are things that happened to other people and not themselves. That old "There but for the grace of God go I" mentality can be utilized by a gossip as easily as by anyone else.

One constant human foible that isn't likely to change is that we like to tell things about one another. Some people are extremely more proficient in this regard than others and I've known some world-class gossips in my time. Folks who, when practically any name comes up, can promptly supply a bit of personal negativity. A failing. A crime. Maybe just a little stumble along life's road. Anything at all will suffice for a gossip. And, ironically, this is usually someone who will rant loudly against the practice and even throw in a little scripture about judging others lest ye be judged.

If I ever get to be king, I'll do away with gossiping entirely. Not little morsels of harmless information that happen to come my way, you understand. Just the hurtful, mean-spirited things. Just the tired, old, dredged up snippets of other peoples' business that are best left in the past.

Because I agree with Mark Twain, who maintained that "it takes your enemy and your friend, working together, to hurt you to the heart; the one to slander you and the other to get the news to you."

I guess you knew that Mark Twain was probably an atheist. And he declared bankruptcy at least once.

I didn't know if you knew that.

Oscar woes

I am writing this on Monday, January 22. Which means that, this time tomorrow, I will almost certainly be disappointed, not to mention more than a little put out.

Because tomorrow morning, on the twenty-third, the Academy of Motion Picture Arts and Sciences will announce this year's nominees for the Oscars, those highly coveted bald-headed statues that are supposed to denote excellence in the world of the movies.

And, unless this year is different from most others, I won't agree with most of the selections, if any.

Now, if I thought there was any possibility that you'd believe that I am actually writing this on the twenty-second (which I am), I'd make a few predictions, just to prove that I rarely agree with the Academy. But there's always the chance, though slight, that I might get a few right. After all—as the old saying goes—even a blind hog finds an acorn now and again. And then you'd say I'd cheated, and sent this to the paper after the announcement. Or—and this is the most likely scenario—I wouldn't get anything right and you'd chalk me up as an imbecile when it comes to knowing anything about what makes a good performance or a good movie.

But I know what I like. And, that being the only light I have to navigate by, it will just have to suffice.

It's not like I approach these selections from total ignorance. My wife, Karen, and I go to the movies pretty often, on the average of once a week. So we see something like forty-five or so films

in any given year. And I have old favorites—bona fide classics—
that I can watch over and over and use as reference points. Like
In Harm's Way. When I churn through the channels and come
across that flick, I'm good for a couple of hours.

Needless to say, *In Harm's Way* didn't win any Oscars, and
probably wasn't nominated for any. Which wasn't the first time,
by a long shot, that the Academy got it wrong.

In 1939, a year in which Hollywood produced a bumper crop
of fine films, *The Wizard of Oz* lost out to *Gone With the Wind*.
A closer call than many, I agree, but *The Wizard of Oz* was hands-
down the better of the two. And, in 1952, a year that saw the
arrival of not only yours truly but a batch of pretty good movies,
The Quiet Man lost out to Cecil B. DeMille's gaudy circus opus
The Greatest Show on Earth, a miscall on behalf of the Oscar vot-
ers that came close to being a sin.

Sometimes, to be fair, they do get it right. Like they did when
they crowned the first two installments of *The Godfather* trilogy
as Best Picture of their respective years. And, in 1943, they chose
Casablanca. And how could they possibly not have? But even
then they botched it, by picking Paul Lukas as best actor—in
Watch on the Rhine—over Humphrey Bogart, whose turn in
Casablanca might just be the finest performance in the history of
the cinema.

I mean—come on—who even remembers *Watch on the
Rhine*, not to mention Paul Lukas? But "here's lookin' at you,
kid" worked its way immediately into our common language and
is still there more than sixty years later.

So, tomorrow, the Academy will screw up again. And I'll
fume and fuss. I know I said I wouldn't make any predictions and
I won't. But let's just say if Helen Mirren isn't nominated for an
Oscar for *The Queen* and Will Smith for *The Pursuit of
Happyness* [sic], then they might as well quit giving them.

But, I've said that before, about countless other actors and other movies. And usually my predictions come up short on announcement day. Because until the Academy finally sees the light and lets me pick the winners—or, at the very least, the nominees— they are doomed to selecting the wrong films and actors. Sometimes, I think they pick whoever's picture has been splashed most often on the cover of *People* magazine.

In the morning, it wouldn't surprise me if they nominated Paris Hilton for something. After all, as Bogie famously said, "we'll always have Paris."

And, these days, it looks like he might have been right.

The ties that bound
two complete strangers

So, there were these two men—one in southern California and the other on the Texas Gulf Coast—who never met. They never corresponded by telephone, telegraph, e-mail, letter, or carrier pigeon. In fact, one of them, almost certainly, never even knew of the existence of the other. How's that for a scenario badly in need of a common thread?

Actually, there were a couple of things these two had in common. I'm one, though I never laid eyes on one of them. And we'll get to the other one shortly.

In 1998, a fellow identifying himself as David Westheimer called me from his home in Los Angeles. A friend had given him a copy of the memoir I'd written about my father and he just wanted to tell me he'd liked it. Since I'd just received a batch of notes from folks who'd taken exception to something I'd written or had been offended by my frequent employment of sentence fragments, I sat down and lapped up this guy's praise like a kitten at a saucer of cream.

It took me a few minutes to realize that I was talking to an author who I had long admired. His novel *Von Ryan's Express*—based loosely on his own experience as a prisoner of war in WWII—is masterful, and it was made into a top-notch film with Frank Sinatra. Another fine book of his was *My Sweet Charlie*, which became a television movie with Patty Duke.

That first visit went well enough after we got past the manda-
tory niceties, and we started e-mailing each other pretty regularly.
About whatever we were working on at the time. About the status
of literature and politics and the world in general. We sent photographs of our families back and forth, and birthday greetings.
Each December I got a Christmas card and he got one for
Hanukkah. We were comfortable with each other, I guess you
could say, though we were something of an odd couple: an
eighty-something author who hadn't had a bestseller in a half
century, and a forty-something one who never had one at all.
David was a mentor for me, though half a continent separated us,
and I suppose I was a sounding board for him.

Victor Platt was my mentor also. And I knew him considerably longer than I knew David. In 1981, I took a teaching job at
the high school where Victor taught drama and senior English;
he took me under his wing, and over the next two decades we
became close friends. I taught his daughters; he proofread my
first, very bad manuscripts. He was perhaps the most gifted nat-
ural teacher I've ever known, and he held his students spellbound.

He held me spellbound, as well. And the countless hours that
we spent talking about books and writing and movies and a hundred other things was not just time well spent. It was priceless. If
I amount to anything as either a teacher or a writer, it is in no
small part owing to Victor.

That second common dominator that linked these two
strangers was that they were both amazing practitioners—one as
a writer and the other as a teacher—of wordsmithing, which is
the art of selecting the very best word and phrase in every situation.

When *Writer's Digest* asked me, a few years ago, to write a
book about the use of setting and description for their *Write*

Great Fiction series, I made sure this was on the dedication page: "For Victor Platt and David Westheimer. Wordsmiths, both."

I would have liked to have added, in their personal copies, that they were friends and mentors, also. But they were both gone by then.

Neither of them had much time left when we had our last visits, David by e-mail and Victor, just a week before his death, over the phone from his hospital room in Houston. No time was wasted in either conversation on what we meant to each other, because we already knew that. It was a given, in both relation-ships, and didn't need to be said out loud.

The subject was books in both of those final visits. Books we'd read and books we intended to read. In each conversation, the knowledge that I would have to do all the reading now was left unsaid.

When David and Victor left, my world became smaller, as worlds are apt to do when essential things are removed. I could get sappy now, about how much I miss them and our time together.

But they wouldn't have stood for any such mushiness. Which is one more thing they had in common.

Storytelling

I sometimes kid myself into thinking, when somebody tells me they enjoyed one of my novels, that their enjoyment was owing to my excellent description, believable dialogue, and clever wording. When, in reality, it was the story they liked. And, almost always, the story that a writer tells is his or her take on a story that has been told countless times before.

That's not to say that all those other devices and manipulations aren't important to the writing and to its ultimate effect on the reader. But description and clever syntax and witty, sharp dialogue and many other manipulations that a good writer employs—like a magician pulling rabbits out of a hat—are like the attractive parts of a car. And the story is the engine. It's nice to have lots of doodads and shiny chrome and glossy paint on a car. But, first and foremost, you'd better have an engine. The same goes, when it comes to writing, for a good, dependable story. Because that's what keeps your reader or listener onboard.

You want proof?

Let's go to the first section of the Bible. Not for any spiritual nurturing, though it is there in abundance. This time, let's consider the Old Testament solely as reading material. Anyone intending to read the Bible through—from Genesis to Revelation—is likely to start out swimmingly. They will probably churn right through Genesis and Exodus. But many a well-intentioned reader has skidded to a stop a couple of pages into Leviticus.

Here's why. Genesis and Exodus are full of stories, and mighty fine ones. What with that Adam/Eve/snake triangle, Noah and his floating zoo, Abraham folding up his tent and taking off to parts unknown, and Moses pulling down all those plagues. That's good stuff. Then, in Leviticus, there are suddenly no stories at all. There's a long, dry catalogue of rules.

I may need the rules. But I'll more willingly swallow the stories.

Who among us doesn't have good memories of great storytellers in our lives? Maybe it was a grandparent or an uncle who could spin a yarn as smoothly as buttermilk oozing out of a porcelain cup. Maybe it was a teacher who made history come completely alive by turning dusty, old facts into a tale full of living, breathing people.

The Library of Congress and National Public Radio have always realized the power of stories and, within the last few years, they've teamed up to harvest a bunch of them. They call this adventure Storycorps, and it involves putting a recording studio housed in a trailer at various places around the country. It's a simple enough process. Two people—maybe a mother and daughter, a father and son, old friends—go in, sit down, and one asks a couple of questions to get the other one started. Then a story emerges. Finally, those stories end up in the audio archives of the Library of Congress, where they become individual threads of the rich, enormous tapestry that is our history. And our soul.

NPR plays one every Friday morning, and I listen to it on my way to work. A couple of weeks ago, one Mrs. Theresa Burroughs told her daughter how, in a city in the deep south in the early 1960s, she learned how to play dominoes by having to stand waiting while the white men at the voter registration table finished their games before asking her ridiculous questions that she couldn't possibly answer. Questions that were designed to keep her from registering to vote. Like how many black jelly beans were in a large jar on the table. She kept going back, day after day, and the men finally made the mistake of asking her to recite the preamble to the Constitution, which she did perfectly. And so she voted, that day, for the first time.

That story, told by a persistent woman who I would be proud to know, speaks infinitely louder and clearer about the ignorance of prejudiced people and the inherent evil of discrimination than any statute banning the "N" word ever could.

Because stories are powerful, powerful things. They are the ties that bind us tightly to our past and, hopefully, they are the warnings that occasionally tap us on our collective shoulder and keep us from repeating our foolishness.

So, you heard any good stories lately?

I certainly hope so.

Regarding greener pastures
and
unsmelled roses

We used to have a framed cross-stitch in our house that said "Bloom Where You're Planted." My wife brought it along into our marriage, along with three little girls, some nice antiques, and a car that didn't run very well.

I liked that picture, but I've come to the conclusion that much of modern society doesn't follow its excellent advice very often or very well.

Here's an example. By the time the paper you're reading this in plops into your yard, it might be eighty degrees outside. But as I write it, I'm waiting for sunshine to peek out of gray, low clouds for the first time in I don't know how many chilly, dreary days. You might remember that not too many weeks ago the subject of this diatribe was how much I was looking forward to the first big blue norther of the year. Well, I can now report, after more winter than we're used to on the Gulf Coast, that I am hungry for warm weather.

If truth be known, I spend too much of my time during the mosquito-infested, humid days of summer dreaming of a crackling fireplace, a snug armchair, and winter skies filling up the windows. Then, when I actually have those things, I tend to want nothing more than bright sunny days and temperatures topping eighty-five.

I do believe it is a common peculiarity of human beings to yearn for a season they are not currently in.

And this goes for the seasons of our lives as well as the seasons of the calendar year. Think of the kid in seventh or eighth grade who wants nothing more than to move up to high school. After all, high school is cool—to their way of thinking—and intermediate school is old hat. Then, when he or she gets to high school they discover that they, who might have been the lead dog across town, are mighty small potatoes all of a sudden.

Now that I've mixed more metaphors than I can even keep up with, let's move this kid along to his or her senior year, where they might have to spend a lot of their time in English IV with yours truly.

It's downright pitiful when I get a student whose whole focus is on the college they'll be going to the next year. Sometimes that seemingly greener pasture pulls so hard that they've mentally left the rest of us completely behind: friends and teachers and activities that could have been meaningful and even enjoyable if they hadn't been so far above and beyond them.

I'll make a wager that kids like that won't like college either, but will have their sights entirely set on getting out and into a workforce that isn't likely to please them one bit. They'll count the years and then the months and then the days till retirement. Then, when they retire, they'll be restless and unhappy and bored. But they'll be at the last station on the line by then, and all of their life will have been spent wanting something else. Something better. Something bigger.

Then, they may wish they'd paid attention in senior English class when we did the poem that says to "gather ye rosebuds while ye may." They might wish, too late, that they had slowed down and enjoyed life as it presented itself.

In short, they should have bloomed where they were planted, at each and every stage of their lives.

A few years ago my sister Diane—a cheerful grandmother who never meets a stranger and usually makes them smile—and I sat in lawn chairs at the beach and watched a fine sunset after a wonderful day in which our families had enjoyed good food, good fellowship, and good memories.

"You know," Diane said, "I could stay in a day like this forever."

It reminded me of the line from Truman Capote's *A Christmas Memory*, when a character announces that, "As for me, I could leave the world with today in my eyes."

Now that's blooming where you're planted. That's taking every moment and day and season as it comes and getting the absolute most out of it that it has to offer.

Personally, I intend to try to do better at that. And I will, if this darned cold weather will get along and some long overdue sunshine will break through.

Islands in the stream
of consciousness

I'm in Bermuda.

It's Thursday, February 15, the temperature is hovering around seventy-four delightful degrees, the bright sun is hindered by only a few small white pillows of clouds, and I just enjoyed a good lunch of shepherd's pie and a pint in a waterfront pub. That's Castle Harbor out there, just beyond that cobblestone street meandering beneath tall palm trees swaying in the sea breeze. All the cottages and bungalows hereabouts are painted every pastel hue imaginable, which seems awfully unBritish for a British colony, but it's the custom here. At the mouth of the harbor, the slowly approaching surf works past little Nonsuch Island, darker water swirls over the reefs, and then there's nothing but the wine-dark, brooding Atlantic stretching out to the horizon.

Now, anyone who knows that I am a public school teacher probably realizes that I am not actually in Bermuda. Not in mid-February. Not with the all-holy, all-important TAKS state test looming large and close, and not on a teacher's pay.

I am, in fact, at my keyboard in my office that used to be a bedroom in our house at 4:30 A.M. on a day that the weatherman predicts won't climb out of the forties. He said a few flakes of snow might even materialize.

But the central character in the novel I've been working on since July *is* in Bermuda. So that means that I have to be, as well. At least in my imagination.

So, while I've been working on that section of the book—three chapters—that transpires on that tiny cluster of claw-like islands in the middle of the ocean, my desk has disappeared under a couple of large maps spread out wide, two open guide books, and several articles I dug up. I've Google-Earthed the islands so many times, dropping in from my satellite perspective and scanning roads and beaches and harbors, that I'm pretty certain I'll be able to find my way around if I actually do go there one day.

I don't know if most other writers become as entrenched in the sensory details and the logistics of a setting as I do. But I'd bet on it. How else, if they didn't, would they be able to deliver the place to the reader at all?

This total immersion into another time and/or place occurs to varying degrees in every writing project I undertake, but never to the extent that it did when I wrote *The Windows of Heaven*, set in Galveston during the 1900 storm. I wrote that book a full century after the events of the story, which meant that while most of the world was focused on the approaching millennium and worrying about Y2K, I was—in my head, at least—listening to the clip-clopping of horses pulling buggies and wagons along Broadway (a grand total of three automobiles were registered in Galveston in 1900) and gazing out at a harbor full of tall-masted wooden ships from all over the world, most of their holds full of Mr. Moody's cotton.

Before I wrote one word of that book, I read everything I could get my hands on about the island and her storm. I walked the streets of Galveston countless times, looking for buildings that survived, and standing on street corners to get the angles right. I must have watched two old movies—*A Tree Grows in Brooklyn* and *O'Henry's Full House*—twenty times each, to actually see and hear what things were like in cities at the turn of that century.

I stood for long periods of time on the seawall beside Wal-Mart, which sits on the site of an orphanage that is a major setting in the story, and tried hard to imagine what the place looked like when William McKinley was president and Queen Victoria and Mark Twain were still alive.

In other words, I had to go to Galveston in 1900. In my mind.

So, you might be wondering why I don't just go to Bermuda and spend a few days, to get the feel of the place.

I guess you weren't paying attention about the teacher's pay.

And, like I constantly tell my students, a good writer doesn't have to actually visit a place in order to describe it. Ray Bradbury, I remind them, never went to Mars, but his rendering of Martian mountains and plains is some of the best stuff in literature.

Now, if you'll excuse me, I think I'll order a coffee before I quit this pub and make my way over to Prince of York Street. I'm considering buying a pair of Bermuda shorts in a shop on King's Square.

Animals

The fact that four cats live in my house seems to confuse as many people as it impresses. When I relate a tale about Will, Grace, Missy, and Earl Gray, or write about them in the paper, the response varies from "I love cats" to "I'm just not a cat person" to a blank stare not unlike the much overused simile involving a deer in the headlights.

It's that last group that I pity. Because they just don't get it.

The other two camps, cat lovers and cat avoiders, are right up front about which bandwagon they are on. And, even if they don't care for cats, it doesn't necessarily mean they don't harbor an affinity for some other branch of the vast animal kingdom. But it might.

And that would be a shame.

Somebody told me once that he loved animals, but just the ones he could shoot. It didn't get the laugh he wanted. In fact, it didn't get a laugh at all. All I could think was that he'd best not use that line around my wife.

Because my wife is a sort of one-woman crusade when it comes to the proper care and treatment of just about every creature in creation. Karen will feed anything that wanders up, will forego the enjoyment that a circus has to offer by worrying about how the lions and tigers and bears are being treated, and is fit to be tied when she hears about how somebody has tortured a cat or a dog or starved a horse or . . . well, you get the idea.

When we first got married, an old black cat named Stormy came along as part of the deal. We didn't like each other at first, but we got to be pals. So much so that when Stormy got so old and feeble that she had to be put down, it was a heck of a lot harder on me than I ever would have believed.

Before Stormy and I befriended each other, Karen had told me that cats were good company and excellent stress relievers. I didn't believe her, of course. But now I do. Now I realize that when the strain and folly of the world starts closing in, the fellowship of animals can be downright therapeutic.

For instance, let's say I come home after an exasperating day, one full of what Mr. Shakespeare called the slings and arrows of outrageous fortune. One full of nothing going right. I thumb through the mail—seven bills and a jury duty summons—I reach for a cold beverage but we're all out, and I plop down in my chair and turn on the evening news. Which is all bad.

And there on the ottoman by my feet is Grace, the smallest of our quartet of felines and the one most devoted to yours truly. Gracie doesn't care a fig about all those things that have got me in a bad mood. All she cares about, at the moment, is me. And that's comforting. Okay, to be fair she also cares about the treats that I keep on the end table that I feed to her when she has been especially considerate and attentive. Today she gets three.

Gracie and I are pretty far removed from each other on the biological family tree. But it's nice to know that, for a few minutes, at least, we are kindred spirits. For a little while, it is Gracie and me against the world.

I am in complete agreement with Henry Beston, who wrote a little book in 1928 that ranks pretty high on my list of all-time favorites. It's called *The Outermost House* and it is his memoir of spending a full calendar year on Cape Cod's Great Beach.

He hit the nail on the head when he said we need "another and a wiser and perhaps a mystical concept of animals." He maintained that "the animal shall not be measured by man. In a world older and more complete than ours they move finished and complete, gifted with extensions of the senses we have lost or never attained, living by voices we shall never hear. They are not our brethren, they are not underlings; they are other nations, caught with ourselves in the net of life and time, fellow prisoners of the splendor and travail of the earth."

Other nations. I like that, and so does Gracie. I just read it to her, and gave her a treat. Whereupon she purred, blinked, and gave me an appreciated gaze full of love and devotion.

"A car is a car is a car" didn't drive my father

On my way to work one foggy morning a couple of weeks ago I got caught at a red light behind an old Buick LeSabre, a late '60s or early '70s model. I can't give you a specific year because I've never been one of those guys who can rattle off the makes and models of cars. My interest in automobiles is completely utilitarian; if it is comfortable, has a radio that picks up the Astros, meets my wife's aesthetic criteria, and starts up when I turn the key it's fine by me.

So, here I was at that traffic light with this wide, sleek LeSabre idling away in her old age, and I thought of my father.

He bought three LeSabres back when I was in high school and college and just starting my long sentence as a public school teacher. Now I don't want to give you the impression that he had a whole fleet. We were a one car family, if you don't count the school car, which is what we called the old army surplus, olive-drab sedan that was at the disposal of my father, in his capacity as the school superintendent in Oakwood, the little East Texas town where I grew up. What I should have made clear a few sentences ago was that he bought those Buicks one after the other, over a period of probably fifteen years.

He was that loyal to that one product and to a few others as well. For instance, he drank only Schlitz and Jax beer. Both of which, I believe, have gone out of business, and not because my father's death cut very deeply into their profits. He drank a couple of cans a week, maybe one or two more than that in the hot summertime when we mowed the yard.

I, being in high school—more accurately, I should say being in his eyesight—didn't drink any beer during those yard mowings. I had to settle for a cold glass of Cragmont cream soda. My father was also loyal to the generic brands of products in the Safeway store in Palestine where we bought our groceries every Saturday afternoon. So we drank Cragmont drinks instead of Cokes and Dr Peppers and ate Lucerne mellorine instead of ice cream. Those of you who don't know what mellorine was, be thankful. Let's just say it was about as much like real ice cream as I am like Brad Pitt.

It was never any mystery why my father bought the Safeway products. He was thrifty. Which, of course, is the polite way of saying he was cheap. Not cheap in the sense that my mother or my sisters or I ever wanted for anything we really needed. But economical, to the point of driving across Palestine to the Piggly Wiggly to save a few pennies on a jar of jelly.

But I've never figured out why he shifted his allegiance, sometime about 1968, from Chevrolet Impalas to Buick LeSabres. I grew up riding in Impalas; he had three of them, one at a time. Then, for whatever reason, he became a LeSabre man.

Buick advertisements wouldn't have enticed him; he wasn't the type to be swayed by a commercial. Neither would an article in *Consumer Reports*. His reading was limited strictly to the daily newspapers from Palestine, Dallas, and Houston and an occasional article in *The Saturday Evening Post* or *Reader's Digest* that my mother suggested. I'm pretty sure he read only one novel in his lifetime. It was *Bonney's Place* by Leon Hale, the *Houston Chronicle* columnist who then wrote for the now defunct *Post*. I told Mr. Hale once that if he had written a new translation of the *Odyssey*, my father would have read that, too.

Because he was loyal to Leon Hale, you see. And, to my father, loyalty to important things—like God, family, and country—was essential. And loyalty to lesser things—like brands of beer, automobiles, mellorine, and favorite journalists—was a good indication of fidelity and sound judgment.

The God, family, and country (and, I admit it, Leon Hale) part worked its way down into me, and I'm glad it did. But the devotion to particular brands didn't. Ketchup is ketchup, as far as I'm concerned. But my father would have passed up fried potatoes altogether if he didn't have a bottle of Heinz close at hand.

I had forgotten that about him until I pulled up behind an old car at a stop light one foggy morning. So, if that LeSabre belongs to you, thanks for the memory.

A fine lady,
a little town,
and a great big legacy

Here goes a totally inadequate attempt to say goodbye to my friend Janice Eubank, who was a textbook example of a master teacher, a constant lover of life, and a courageous fighter.

She was a proud daughter of Tulia, who left that tiny burg a long time ago and went home for good last week.

I never heard her say "I'm from a little town near Amarillo," or "I'm from the panhandle." It was always "I'm from Tulia," boomed out in a confident, determined voice.

One summer, I tagged along on one of the many trips on which she took her students to Washington DC. Janice believed that every American should visit our capital city and, since I hadn't, she shamed me into going. One hot day, our tour bus broke down in a seedy neighborhood. While we waited beside the street for another bus to come and collect us, one of the kids took a look around and said she sure wouldn't want to live there. Another student said it wasn't any worse than where he was from.

Whereupon Janice, her nose already in the city map and planning our next stop, cast one of her pearls. "Don't ever be ashamed of where you came from," she said, "just don't let it keep you from where you're going." Then she slapped the map shut—everything she did was so full of energy that I sometimes got exhausted just watching her—and looked up the street for that new bus.

She was always looking for something. A new way to teach a lesson, a new place to eat, a new cake recipe that she could whip up and bring to the teachers' workroom, a new town in the Hill Country to explore.

This was a lady who truly made an effort to get the most out of each and every day. And there's just not a lot of folks that I can say that about. She could thoroughly enjoy an Italian opera in Houston and, later that night, have a great time two-stepping to country music.

She decided she wanted to be a teacher when she was still a little girl, out there in Tulia. And she never wavered from the plan. She started teaching in the early 1960s and she kept at it well past when she could retire with full benefits. In fact, when she had stayed longer than her health had, we thought we'd have to change the lock on her classroom door to make her stay home and rest.

But she didn't want to rest. She wanted to teach. She was my colleague for over twenty years, and I don't believe I've ever seen anyone who honestly loved the profession as much as she did. She was almost always the first teacher to arrive in the morning and often the last to leave in the afternoon. She served on count-less committees, was the chair of the social studies department, and was elected the district's Teacher of the Year. But honors and committees weren't nearly as important to her as when she stood up in front of her class and did what she knew that she had been built to do.

Her students were fortunate to have crossed her path. And so were her friends. I counted myself one of those, and I'll always be grateful for it.

In all the years I knew her, the only thing close to a disagree-ment that we ever had was over homemade chili. I put beans in mine, and Janice maintained that real Texans just don't do that. So she was quick to tell me, and quick, literally, as she told me. Sometimes she'd get to talking so fast that her listeners would lean forward, as if being pulled along in her wake.

She talked like she lived, at full throttle.

In fact, I never saw anything slow her down until she got Lou Gehrig's disease. When she had to start using a wheelchair, we knew that it was bad. Then, when that fine, quick mind started going, we knew that it was only a matter of time.

The time finally came last week.

She was a proud daughter of Tulia. And Tulia can be mighty proud of her.

Lest we forget

The construction of a veterans' memorial has been a hot topic lately. Not so much about whether or not one is needed—after all, being against a veterans' memorial would be sort of like coming out against racial tolerance and world peace—but about what sort of thing it would end up being.

Now, I'm a veteran myself, so I perk up and pay attention when this subject arises. After all, this is likely to be the only memorial that will ever be put up to yours truly other than a tombstone. And I'll gladly do without that one for as long as possible.

Uncle Sam sent his greetings to me in the early '70s, informing me I'd be spending two years on his meal ticket. I was in college at the time, though hardly on the Dean's List. In fact, the only list the dean had which my name might have been on would have been of students in need of a little pep talk concerning grades. But the Selective Service System got a look at those grades first, and I ended up raising my hand and reciting the oath that delivered me into the Army of the United States.

The Vietnam War was in its last gasps, so I ended up in Germany, which was fine by me. I was all of twenty, had never wandered very far away from East Texas, and there I was deep in the Black Forest in Bavaria. I was a clerk–typist in a machine shop, saw enough sights and learned enough history to make me more well-rounded and drank enough rich German beer to make me physically so well-rounded that my family had trouble recognizing me when I got home.

Not all who served—draftees or by choice—fared nearly as well. Believe me, I know that. But even those of us who were never in harm's way pulled on the uniform every day and put our lives on hold for a while. Every veteran everywhere deserves to be acknowledged. They did their bit. They might very well have bellyached about it and might have resented every day of it. But they stepped up to the plate.

And far too many, of course, *have* been in harm's way.

I don't need to go into the sacrifices that countless American veterans have made throughout our history. I've strolled among rows upon rows of white tombstones at the cemetery at Omaha Beach in Normandy, most of which bear the same date: June 6, 1944. Most of which contain the bodies of kids barely older than the ones I teach in my high school senior English class. And I have seen the flags flapping in the breeze along the streets in my town way too often lately, indicating that one of our own died in a war that is currently a topic of hot debate and is now fodder for presidential campaigns.

But here's what we all ought to try to remember. The debate on that—or any—war, or the concept of war in general, whatever our stand on it, has not one thing to do with the people, almost all of them awfully young, who have to do the actual waging of war. Our troops in the field, past and present, should be completely outside the realm of politics and philosophy and partisanship. They should be considered only in the light of support, honor, and gratitude.

So, am I in favor of a veterans' memorial?

You bet I am. It needn't involve the changing of the names of streets or existing parks; the names of those places are part of the established fabric of a community, and should, in my opinion, be left alone. This memorial could be a plaza or a courtyard, or maybe a series of smaller efforts throughout town. Maybe one place—with a plaque and a bench—for each branch of the service. Or one for each of our wars.

Or it might be something altogether different that I, having not one whit of experience in planning memorials, could ever envision.

But, whatever this memorial ends up being, it should pale in comparison to the constant gratitude that we express to those who are now serving and those who have served in the past.

The collective, heartfelt "thank you" of a grateful nation—which many veterans of the Vietnam War never received when they came home—would be a finer and more fitting monument than any physical structure we could build.

The devil's not the only thing in the details

So, are you up to participating in a couple of experiments? I have my students at writing conferences do these to improve their memory and attention to detail—essential tools for writers. And even if you have no intention of taking a stab at writing, they might just improve yours, too.

Who couldn't do with a better memory and seeing things more accurately?

The first one I call Focus on the Present. And it involves plopping yourself down, with a notepad and a pencil, in a busy place that you don't visit very often. So where you work is off limits. So is any room in your house. And remember, I said it has to be busy. Which means there has to be enough going on for you to have lots of details to harvest. An airport waiting area is a good choice, or a bench in a crowded mall.

Then, here's what you do. Jot down as many sensory particulars as you can locate from your vantage point. You'll be amazed at the little things you'll notice when you're really paying attention. And don't just scribble down what you see. Most beginning writers load up all their description in only one of the five senses and pass up hearing, smelling, tasting, and feeling. When you get home, take out your notes and do your best to capture the place in a page or two of good description.

The second variation of this assignment—and most folks' favorite—is called Focus on the Past. This time, you don't have to go anywhere; all you have to do is sit down, close your eyes, and remember a specific place.

There are two nonnegotiable rules for this one. First, you have to select a place that you haven't been to in at least ten years, minimum, but that you remember well enough to be able to recall the details. Why not push the envelope here and make it thirty or forty years? Your grandmother's living room might work fine. Or maybe the back yard of the house you grew up in. How about your fifth grade classroom? Or—if there's sufficient mileage on you—the old Coliseum in downtown Houston?

Then, let your mind's eye wander into every corner of that place. Don't bypass a nook or a cranny, a picture on the wall, or a tree in the yard. Which brings us to the second rule: old photos are forbidden. Make your memory do all the work.

One summer I was teaching the memoir workshop at a writer's conference, and one of the participants chose, for this activity, to recall the bridge of the battleship he served on in World War II. The couple of pages of prose that he shared with the group took us all right there to the South Pacific over sixty years ago. We smelled the oil that permeated the whole ship, felt the cold metal of the gauges and instruments, heard the sad lament of the fog-horn bellowing off into the night, and tasted the strong coffee that the officers were served in thick ceramic mugs with no handles.

"I'd forgotten about those mugs not having handles," he told us.

Which is the point of the exercise: to remember things that you've forgotten.

This little set of mental calisthenics might jump-start details that your brain has been hording. Just like an old song sometimes does. Or a smell. For me, the aroma of butterbeans boiling puts me right back in my long-gone grandmother's kitchen in Livingston, where I do believe she cooked butterbeans every day.

So consider taking a stroll down memory lane. It'll be fun, and it might even prove to be profitable.

One time I had a student who chose to remember the guest room in her former mother-in-law's house. She'd been divorced for ages and hadn't actually been in that room for over twenty years, but, when remembering an ornate old dresser, she recalled putting an expensive ring in one of its tiny drawers for safekeeping during a trip. She hadn't thought of that ring in ages and had long since given it up for lost. Anyway, she called her former husband's mother. Who went upstairs, opened the hidey-hole and—sure enough—there was the ring.

I never found out if the old woman sent it back to her. Which is okay.

Because while precise description is useful to a writer, so is a little mystery.

Yes, we get by with a little help from our friends

Way back when disco was king and Jimmy Carter was the brand new president and Elvis was still in the building, I was a first-year teacher at Palestine High School in the East Texas Piney Woods along with a fellow from Oklahoma named Harold Baade.

We didn't exactly cotton to each other at first, Harold and I, but as that fall semester rolled along we got to be buddies. And by the time we both left Palestine at the end of our third year—him headed back to Oklahoma and me down to the Gulf Coast—we had moseyed over into a bona fide friendship.

We were both bachelors in those days, and we made a pact before we drove in opposite directions out of that little town, pledging that we would work at keeping the friendship alive. And we did, for a good long while. Harold would come down to visit in the summers and I made a couple of trips up there. We called each other on the phone pretty regularly, even when phones had cords and were tethered to walls.

Then the years started piling up and we both got married and the visits dried up to none at all and then the phone calls did, too. Which is embarrassing and unforgivable. After all, how difficult is it to make a phone call?

Harold and I let that good friendship sputter out like an engine that finally runs out of gas.

What reminded me of this were two outstanding books that I've recently read and that I highly recommend: *Franklin and*

Winston: An Intimate Portrait of an Epic Friendship and *Grant and Twain: The Story of a Friendship that Changed America.*

Now, before you go thinking I'm comparing Harold and me to Franklin Roosevelt, Winston Churchill, Ulysses Grant or Mark Twain, let me assure you that I'm not (though Harold is beginning to look a little like Churchill, now that I think of it).

It was fate that threw Roosevelt and Churchill together, as leaders of two nations that had to take on Mr. Hitler, the determined bully of that era. And it was a business deal—the publication of Grant's memoirs—that united the creator of Huckleberry Finn and the former president.

But the enduring alliances that grew from those associations went far beyond government and business. These were men who discovered that they enjoyed being in each other's company. Like Harold and I do.

The two of us never got around to saving the free world or changing the face of American literature. We just pretty much went to Astros games and movies and found good places to eat and sat on porches and patios and watched the world slide by.

But the glue that held our friendship together was the same one that worked for those other, more famous ones: a rich mixture of common respect, trust and camaraderie. More than that, it was the comfortable knowledge that we didn't have to work at impressing each other.

Maybe you are half of a friendship that strong. I hope so.

It was Mr. Shakespeare who offered some sound advice about this. In *Hamlet,* he has Polonius say this: "Those friends thou hast, and their adoption tried, grapple them unto thy soul with hoops of steel."

Which means, I'm pretty sure, that if you are lucky enough to have stumbled into a friendship that is rock solid, you'd better hang on to it and do the necessary maintenance to keep it going.

And, as was usually the case, Will hit the nail on the head.

Now, if you'll excuse me, I need to give old Harold a call up there in Oklahoma. It's been way too long since we visited. I should be the one to break the silence, since he called me the last time, and since "friendship" is the state motto of Texas. My research team (Google.com) tells me that the state motto of Oklahoma is "labor conquers all things." Which lends no weight to this matter whatsoever.

I'll bet you've got a friend out there somewhere that you need to reconnect with. So put down the paper and do it. I shouldn't have to remind you and neither should Mr. Shakespeare.

The write stuff

It's the middle of April, which means professional baseball is in full swing, school students and their teachers are in the home-stretch toward summer vacation, cantaloupes are getting sweeter, and—for those of us who are into yarn-spinning—writers' conferences are dotting our calendars like spring calves in fields of clover.

I get asked to speak and lead workshops at conferences because I'm not important enough of a writer to do much damage to their budgets. And probably because I look so little like an author that prospective scribblers can take one glance at me and figure that if I could get published then there is hope for anyone.

I like conferences. I get to learn a trick or two from other writers, get a free lunch, and meet interesting people. Having gone to a good many now, I've determined there are generally three groups who attend.

One is made up of folks who are dipping their toes in the waters of creativity for the first time. They love to read and figure they'll love to write. Probably their wife or husband or somebody else has pushed them in the direction of the conference and might have even signed them up and paid their registration as a gift so they'll have to actually go.

I call this the "Pardon me, I really shouldn't be here" crowd. They are friendly and almost always shy and reserved, as if they are marching under a false flag, feeling as out of place as a Democrat at a Lincoln Day dinner. What usually happens is that, at the end of the day, they either leave telling themselves that they'll actually begin writing something one of these days or they catch on fire like a convert at a tent revival and buy every book about writing they can locate and go home and write up a storm, churning out reams of pages of what they intend to be the great American novel.

I call the second group—located at the other end of the spectrum from the "Pardon Me" crowd—the "Show ME the Money" herd. They have absolutely no interest in learning how to write better or how to create believable characters or settings or plots. Their one and only concern is how to make a lot of cash at this writing racket.

These people are in a hurry to learn the great secret so they can be on their way. They are not into chit-chat or mixing and, when I tell them that one look at my bank account would convince them that there is absolutely nothing I can tell them about making a lot of money at writing, they look positively put out, like I've deemed them unworthy of sipping from the Holy Grail. Then, when I refuse to give them the phone number of my literary agent, they stomp off to find a more knowledgeable and accommodating writer.

Finally, most of the participants at conferences fall into the third group, which I call the "Eyes on the Prize" section. They are currently working on something—a novel or a short story or a memoir or some poems—and have already started collecting their letters of rejection from publishers. Sometimes I tell them about the shoebox full of rejections I got before I sold my first book. Then I tell them that persistence does, sometimes, pay off.

The "Eyes on the Prize" bunch is grateful for any advice that comes their way regarding writing. When I tell them to keep going into lonely rooms and sitting down to keyboards and practicing the art of wordsmithing—choosing the right words, like selecting perfect pebbles for a mosaic—they nod and I realize they know exactly what I'm talking about. The "Pardon Me" sect must wonder at such a ritual, and the "Show Me the Money" clan sees no merit at all in actually laboring over a manuscript. They just want to know how and where to peddle it when it magically emerges.

If you are in the "Eyes on the Prize" or the "Pardon Me" groups, I'd love to see you at a conference. They're great places to meet published writers and, occasionally, agents and editors. But, more important, they are the best places to meet other folks just like you, people feeling their way through stories and characters and looking for good advice.

If our paths cross at one, stop by to say hello and tell me what you're working on. But don't ask for my agent's phone number.

The picture show

Today we're at the movie theatre. More accurately, we're at a concrete beehive containing multiple movie theatres.

The film's not too bad. But the guy behind me is explaining everything in the story to his wife as his knees jab away at the back of my seat. The place is packed, making relocation not an option. So the twelve bucks I shelled out for us to get in here is just going to have to buy his running commentary as a bonus.

It's times like this when I have to wonder how long it will be before movie theatres will be things of the past. When it seems certain that the day can't be far off when I'll be able to punch a few buttons on my TV remote control and order any movie I want. I'm not talking about the limited selection of titles in the cable company's repertoire; I mean any movie ever *made*. Even the brand new ones.

Then I won't have to give the bored teenager at the concession counter ten dollars for snacks and soda that would set me back all of maybe two bucks at a grocery store. I'll be able to plop myself down in my favorite chair and enjoy the show without all the cell phones going off and babies crying and sticky residue on the floor and people unwrapping things enclosed in crinkly plastic.

There's somebody going at a cough drop or some candy right now. It is an indisputable law of physics that one old lady in a big theater with a tiny piece of plastic wrapper can make more racket than a marching band.

But, with that big cornucopia of movies at my beck and call and a big screen to watch them on, I'll never have to put up with any of that anymore.

Of course, you are now about to point out that no screen that I could get into my house could ever be as big as the ones in theaters. And you have a point, but not a great one. Television sets are getting so big that architects are designing whole rooms around them. Chances are you already have a set that is many times bigger than the first one you owned. There are probably more total square feet of television screens in America than there are of timberland. (I made that up, but it sounds impressive).

Next you will tell me that nothing can replace the time-honored experience of leaning back in a theater seat and escaping into a fine story splashing out across the big silver screen.

And finally you've hit upon the very reason that movie theaters aren't going anywhere anytime soon. Going to the movies is a ritual woven so tightly into our collective memory and habit that it will be almost impossible to remove it. After all, chances are pretty good that your first date was at a movie theater. And chances are almost as good that you can still name the film.

In Oakwood, the little East Texas town where I grew up, we had a small theatre named the Melba. But we all just called it the picture show. When it closed down we had to drive into Palestine to the bigger, nicer Texas to see movies.

It was in the Texas that my mother became so repulsed at all the blood in *Ben Hur* that she couldn't eat ketchup afterwards on her French fries at Ralph's Drive In. It was also where we saw *Hawaii*, which caused her to call, that very night, the mother of my friend we had taken with us to apologize about the native girls who ran out to meet the missionaries without their shirts on. The native girls, not the missionaries.

And that kid three rows up—the one sneaking his arm around the back of his date's seat—that's me in the Texas in 1968, watching *The Graduate* and hoping the girl will lean a little closer toward me.

It's just too ingrained in us, this going into big rooms with lots of other people and watching flickering images on a wall. New technology isn't likely to stop the ritual. And neither, in spite of all my complaining, are the aggravating details of the experience.

So I'll keep going to the movies. Where I'll just have to put up with the things that get on my nerves. Like the seventeen men and boys in here that are wearing caps.

Excuse me; I just missed part of the film. But no problem, the guy with his knee in my kidneys will bring his gum-popping wife and me up to snuff.

Frozen moments, warm memories, and cold truth

One of the rites of spring has come and gone in my senior English classes. After we finished reading and discussing John Keats's "Ode on a Grecian Urn" I hauled out a bucket of crayons and big sheets of drawing paper and told my students to draw the urn and its illustration that the poet describes in the poem. Down to the last detail.

What the kids came up with is pretty impressive. Two young lovers are in a fond embrace and just about to kiss. A priest is leading a garland-laden heifer to a green alter. A "happy melodist" is "forever piping songs forever new." A river meanders along under a shady bough.

My students have fun with the activity—probably those crayons churn up memories of elementary school—and, hopefully, they get one of Keats's points: that all of the people and things depicted on the urn are frozen in time.

Those two young lovers will always be just about to enjoy the delight of that first kiss. And, because their relationship is unchangeable, they won't have to deal with the pangs of doubt, the first argument, and any other unpleasantness that might come along.

In a perfect time warp, that blissful duo will linger in that wonderful, anticipatory moment. Forever.

In a way, Keats pointed the way toward the marvel of photography, though he predated it by several decades.

Think of the special photographs that you have tucked away somewhere that are real treasures. Now consider why they are such treasures. And I'll bet it's because they offer little windows of frozen time that nothing can tinker with.

On the wall of my study there's a framed photograph of my father walking down a city street. It would have been made not long after World War II when he was in his early forties. He's got on a fedora and is in the process of pulling on his suit coat. His necktie is one of those wide, splashy affairs that men wore then. He's smiling, maybe laughing, and I have no idea what city he is in, who took the picture, where he's been, or where he's going.

And that's the best part. For that split second there is not one indication that he will one day lose his wife and then get Alzheimer's and forget his children. Those tragic episodes are all in the distant future.

But for that one moment—captured on my wall and in my heart—my father is a vibrant, happy man on a street on what looks to be a nice day.

Of course, while I have that framed image and many others of family and friends, there are more famous ones that serve the same purpose. Like the photograph of President Kennedy that was made just a few seconds before he was assassinated. He's smiling, and young, and waving to the crowd, and all that boyish, Camelotish charm glows brightly in the morning sunlight. If he had lived, he would be ninety now. We never got to see the old man that he would have become but were left with the young one that was captured forever on film right before the nation tilted a little on its axis and we lost a good bit of our collective innocence.

I don't show my students either of those pictures—of my father or JFK—when we do "Ode on a Grecian Urn." I'd rather let them focus entirely on the image that Keats described so nicely.

And maybe, if they end up remembering either me or that poem, they might—when they are old and gray and have lived more life than they would ever have thought possible—remember those two young lovers poised forever to plant that first, enchanting kiss.

Then maybe they'll finally agree with Mr. Keats that the meaning of life needn't always be a puzzling thing. That part of the ultimate truth might just be comprised of lots of little beautiful things like frozen images on urns and slips of photo paper.

Maybe they will even recall how he ended that good poem: "Beauty is truth, truth beauty, —that is all ye know on earth, and all ye need to know."

Now, tell the truth. Haven't you ever held up a photograph of yourself taken a long time ago and—just for a moment—you missed that smiling young scamp, frozen in time, that was looking back at you?

Sure you have. And that's part of what Mr. Keats was getting at.

Lonely days and
lonely nights

I've saved today's topic for spring. Because loneliness is definitely a subject that should only be broached in bright sunshine with flowers blooming and birds singing. So, if it's raining and cold outside this morning, at least give me credit for good intentions.

Thank heavens I don't have to deal with being lonely. Not with a wife who also happens to be my best friend, not to mention Will, Grace, Earl Gray, and Missy, our rambunctious feline quartet. But back in my bachelor days there were a few times that I felt like I could have been considered an authority on solitude. And most of those times fell on Sunday afternoons.

I do believe that, back then, Sunday afternoons could be the loneliest times imaginable.

I'm talking around about dusk, when the football or baseball game on television was over and the telephone had been as quiet as a tomb. When there was the gloomy realization that the rest of the world was pretty much shut down. Sometimes Sunday afternoons were like being on the dark side of the moon.

Mondays were a different kettle of fish. Of course, I had to resume serving my life sentence as a public school teacher on most Mondays. But even during summer vacations, Mondays didn't inspire loneliness one bit. On Mondays, and all other weekdays, I knew that the world was up and about its business. Stores and banks and barbeque joints were open. Traffic zipped along, and a fresh batch of bills rattled into my mailbox every day about the same time.

All in all—excepting a few long-ago Sunday afternoons—I've managed to keep loneliness at bay. And I feel sorry for folks who aren't able to.

I've told you before, in this little corner of the paper, about *The Outermost House,* which is one of my favorite books. It's the chronicle of Henry Beston, who spent an entire year in a small cottage on the beach at Cape Cod in the 1920s. Back then, that beach must have been one mighty lonely place, especially during the frigid, bleak winter months. There is much in his narrative about being alone, and I get the strong impression that it proved to be a scary thing indeed.

One of the best quotes about loneliness that my ace research team (Google.com) came up with is attributed to one Charles Caleb Colton, and it made me shudder a little when I read it. Mr. Colton—whoever the heck he was—said "To dare to live alone is the rarest courage; since there are many who had rather meet their bitterest enemy in the field, than their own hearts in their closet."

Think about it. Given the time provided by solitude to give it a close inspection, one's heart might turn out to be a fine thing, full of compassion and optimism and good will. But what if it comes up short? That, to put it mildly, would be a more than a little off-putting.

Before we get overly philosophical here, let me say that it took me a long time to realize a simple truth: that being alone doesn't necessarily mean one has be lonely. I find it amazing that so many people are able to find great strength and purpose in solitude. The author of *The Outermost House* certainly did. And so, of course, did Henry David Thoreau, when he spent that long stretch at Walden Pond.

Such folks find fertile ground in being by themselves, and, sadly, others manage to be terribly lonely even when in a room full of people. So, I'm thinking that solitude depends on how we're individually wired and on each person's unique worldview, and not simply on the number of other human beings that are close by.

Carole Borges, a mighty fine poet, put it like this. "No, my friend; darkness is not everywhere, for here and there I find faces illuminated from within; paper lanterns among the dark trees."

I like that. There are precious few absolutes in life. But one of them has to be that we need more light than darkness, even within the confines of our own hearts and souls. And it's fortunate that the human spirit is sufficiently resourceful to shine in most situations.

Now, if you'll excuse me, Earl Gray's light is shining a little too brightly; he's chasing the other cats through the room. There's about as much chance of being lonely around here as that proverbial snowball has in a place that we'll leave unmentioned, this being a Sunday morning.

One less bookstore

A fairly miraculous thing happened a few summers ago.

During a little short course I was teaching on the writing of fiction, I was giving an example of irony—or conflict or resolution or character description or some other thing from the bag of tricks that I dip into—to my captive audience that was installed comfortably on the chairs and the sofa of Book Ends bookshop. I was using some story from Oakwood, my little hometown in East Texas, to make my point (as I am apt to do pretty often) and one of the participants pointed to something behind me and smiled.

And there, on one of the many brimming shelves of the store, was a small volume with this title on its spine: *Oakwood Methodist Women's Club 1962 Cookbook*. And there, in the soups and salads section, was my mother's recipe for corn chowder.

Oakwood is several hundred miles from Book Ends bookshop, you understand. And 1962 is a long time ago. Which is the miraculous part.

Yet, when I think about it, it really isn't all that miraculous after all. Because Book Ends is the kind of place where such treasures can be found in abundance.

And Becky Dorroh, who runs the place, makes sure the treasure chest is full.

The bad news is that Becky is closing Book Ends on the last day of May, after six years of trying to compete with amazon.com and the big chain stores.

I won't turn this into a diatribe about the national demise of the independent bookseller, or the slow gobbling up of small, friendly, local businesses by corporate monsters. But I will make a prediction: It won't be too long until a locally owned and operated bookshop will be as hard to find as an S&H Green Stamp redemption center. Because they'll be gone with the wind, if I may employ a particularly heavy literary allusion.

And that will be a sad day, indeed. Not only because such stores are likely to have copies of old books that are out of print or hard to locate, but because they almost always have somebody like Becky, who knows about books, cares about them, reads them, and likes to help her customers find them.

The kids they hire at some of the big bookstores don't have any more interest in or knowledge of what they are selling than a check-out clerk at a grocery store has of a can of corn they push under the electronic price reader.

If you ask Becky for the latest P. D. James whodunit, she'll probably either tell you what she thought of it or give you a summary of a review she's read. Then, if she has it in stock, she'll walk you over to it, stepping over several kids sprawled out on the floor reading in the children's section, around one of the two cats—Fia (short for Ophelia) and Princess Buttercup—that live in the store, and past a couple of old friends on the sofa who are catching up on each other's news.

Historians tell us that Abe Lincoln, during the bleakest days of the Civil War—when his generals were losing too many battles, members of his own party were railing against him, and his wife was slipping into severe depression—would sometimes walk down the street from the White House and go into a hardware store. Where he would just stand for a few minutes. If a clerk asked if there was something he could do for him, the president would wave his big hand and tell him "No, son; I just like the smell of the place."

The aroma of leather and metal and musty bins was a comfort to him. Just like the smell of a store containing lots of old books is to me.

So I'll miss Book Ends. And Becky. Though she won't be gone completely, she tells me. She'll maintain her inventory online for internet shoppers.

But she'll be gone, and so will her fine bookshop, when I need to go down there and get a little therapy by smelling the books and handling them. I'll probably feel like old honest Abe without a hardware store to stand in.

Well Pilgrim,
it's time for an awful
big celebration

When I was in the third grade my father loaded the entire popu-
lation of the Oakwood Public Schools—grades one through
twelve—into three school buses and took us to watch *The Alamo.*
My father was the superintendent of schools and was of the opinion that Texas school children could stand a good dose of their
history, even the Hollywood version.

There was no longer a theater—a "picture show" in that
time and place—in Oakwood, so we went to the Rio Theater in
Buffalo, nearly twenty miles away. All of us from Oakwood sat
with the students and teachers from Buffalo in the downstairs
seats, and some of the Buffalo kids had to sit in the small balcony. From which someone emptied the contents of a Coca-
Cola on the head of Miss Lillie Bell Evans, the teacher of the
fifth and six grades in the Oakwood school. This caused the start
of the film to be delayed until Miss Lillie Bell could see to cor-
rections in her hair and makeup and smoke a cigarette to calm
her frazzled nerves and the Buffalo culprit could be located and
whipped.

But finally the lights went down and the big screen flickered
to life and I made the acquaintance, for the very first time, of Mr.
John Wayne. I must admit to being disappointed. For when my
father had told me that Davy Crockett would be in the movie I'd
expected him to be the one that I, outfitted in my coonskin cap
and sitting cross-legged on the linoleum floor, watched on our

black and white Zenith. So when it was not Fess Parker who leaned forward on that horse and delivered Davy's first lines, I had to get used to this new fellow.

On the way back to Oakwood on the bus, I worked up the courage to sit beside Vicky Haney, a girl in my class who was pretty enough in the frilly dresses she came to school in to capture my heart completely.

We watched the late afternoon East Texas landscape—piney woods and pastures and Keechi Creek—slide by outside and I told her I liked Davy Crockett the best in the movie. She looked at me and considered it.

"He's awful *big*," she finally said, not looking at me anymore, but outside again.

I nodded at it, probably. Maybe I said something. Most likely I just looked at her or at her hands. She had pretty little hands.

This was all going on toward half a century ago. I've had other sweethearts, landing finally with the right one that I have had now for a good, long while. Vicky Haney is probably a grandmother somewhere in the world, totally ignorant of the fact that she was ever my sweetheart at all.

But John Wayne is still awful big.

This Saturday, May 26, will be the 100th anniversary of his birth, and, even though he's been dead for nearly a quarter of that time, I believe a celebration is called for.

Big doings are in store lots of places, like the National Cowboy Hall of Fame in Oklahoma City, the John Wayne Cancer Institute in Los Angeles, and at the little white-frame house in Winterset, Iowa, where he was born and christened Marion Morrison, a name he ditched pretty quickly. Surely a bunch of his movies will pop up all over the cable networks, and just as surely more than a few conservative politicians will bloviate about how Duke was the great symbol of the Reagan

Revolution (conveniently forgetting that he was already in his grave before Ronald Reagan became president).

And all of that is fine. And altogether fitting. But my observance will be a significantly quieter affair.

I've determined to select one of Mr. Wayne's many fine films to be representative of his life and work. And I intend to watch that one movie as my official commemoration.

And now, for the hard part: making the right selection. Numerous possibilities spring quickly to mind, but the list would be too lengthy for the space the editor allows me to ramble in. Some worthy contenders are: *She Wore a Yellow Ribbon, In Harm's Way, The Alamo, The Searchers,* and *True Grit.* But on Saturday I'll be watching—drum roll, please—*The Quiet Man.*

And if you're a John Wayne fan, I invite you to select your favorite Duke flick—you have nearly a week to make your choice—and join me in this important celebration. At your own house, of course. I don't have enough popcorn for all of us.

A good man,
an impressive mountain,
and bad shoes

You might remember that our subject several months ago was Colonel E. W. Starling, the central character in the book *Starling of the White House*, which so ably related the heroic exploits of that dashing, long-ago Secret Service agent that it inspired me—as a knobby-kneed, crew-cut lad during the Eisenhower administration—to aspire to become a Secret Service agent myself. Which caused my parents and my sister to stifle their snickers at the dinner table. I finally abandoned the plan. Which was surely a good thing, especially for any future presidents I would have been expected to protect.

Such was the lasting impression of that old book that you are in for another serving of the Colonel today, along with a smidgen about Mount Rushmore.

Last summer, I enjoyed my first trip to that venerable edifice. I'd always wanted to see it, partly because it's something Americans ought to see, and partly because I remembered reading about it in the Colonel's book. Calvin Coolidge, Starling's obvious favorite of the several presidents he served, had his summer White House near there, at the State Game Lodge in Custer State Park.

I am more than moderately interested in presidential history and have read no telling how many biographies of a good many of our chief executives. The best being David McCullough's

John Adams; so if you haven't read it consider that your assignment.

I've always been particularly attracted to Coolidge, who made one of the first presidential gaffes involving a photo-op by allowing himself to be immortalized in an exceptionally grotesque Indian headdress on the White House lawn. The thing was bigger than he was, and he ended up looking like a slender fence post with an eagle's nest crammed on top. My fascination with Mr. Coolidge began with *Starling of the White House*, where I read the Colonel's descriptions of walking along the streets of Washington in the early mornings with Coolidge, who would stop at one of the store windows, look at the displays, and tell the Colonel that, should he ever get married, he shouldn't let his wife go in there. His wife, the president said, went in there pretty often, and it always ended up costing him a lot of money.

That, and when Coolidge released the famous scribbled note to the press announcing that he did not choose to run for reelection. As Starling explained in his book, "to a Vermont Yankee, nothing is more emphatic than 'I do not choose.' It means 'I ain't gonna do it and I don't give a dern what you think.'"

It would be refreshing to hear a politician, these days, state something so categorically. And mean it.

During one of Coolidge's stays in South Dakota, some state officials were so taken with the chief of his Secret Service detail that they decided to name the small valley at the base of Mount Rushmore "Starling Basin." Starling himself called it "a dell of virgin forest lying like a prayer rug before the great shrine of presidents." He was thinking ahead, of course, since at the time only Washington's visage had been carved into the mountain; his three successors still waited in the rock for their liberation.

On the day of my visit to the national monument, I intended to find that place and to think about the good man it was named after. I imagined it as a lonely, beautiful place, with soft wind whispering in the pines and cedars. But I had chosen to wear a pair of leather sandal contraptions that my wife Karen had bought for the trip, and by the time we had tromped down a steep trail to visit several exhibits at the base of the mountain, the giant quartet of dead presidents gazing down at my folly, my feet had been so abused by the instruments of torture that they were in no condition to seek out Starling Basin. So I will have to leave that for another visit.

By that time I will have read *Starling of the White House* yet again. I'm sure of it.

Two ceremonies

It's a Friday night, and I'm settled in at my computer with a glass of milk and a piece of cold chicken, home from my annual participation in a high school commencement ceremony. Since I teach mostly seniors, I always don a robe, process out onto the football field with the kids, and sit with them as they participate in the great sending-off, the dignified ritual.

The problem is—as you'll know, if you've been to one in the last several years—dignity has pretty much fallen by the wayside at these things. They are, these days, more like pep rallies. Or rock concerts. Or NASCAR races.

Now, it's convenient to lay all of the blame on the current crop of youth, and to say that they are all spoiled, have been given way too much, expect to be always entertained, and are unappreciative of the sacrifices made for them. And it's easy enough to get awfully agitated when a good many of them inflate sneaked-in beach balls and send them flying, especially when one gets spiked into the back of my noggin, as was the case tonight.

But that old "youth of today" argument only runs so far, in my opinion. And, lest we forget, it's the same one trotted out by every generation that came before this one.

The vast majority of the kids I taught this year were hardworking, dependable, and altogether fine young people. I was proud to be part of their senior year, and was proud to be part of their graduation, even as rambunctious as it was. They worked hard to get where they are, and I can put up with some of their energetic celebratory behavior at their moment of triumph.

Here's the real problem: the lion's share of the racket tonight came from the *audience*, which provided a continual cacophony of air horns, catcalls, whistles, and a grating caterwauling from some sort of apparatus that, when cranked, sounded like giant cicadas in the throes of a mating ritual. Then whole clans tromped down out of the stands once their own kid's name had been called, laughing and talking while other folks were trying to hear their graduate's recognition.

Now, before you tell me that this is now just the way of the world, and that I should get with the program and lighten up, let me tell you a little story.

Four or five years ago, I was asked by the senior class of a small high school in East Texas to deliver the commencement address. I began with a bit of ancient history; the fact that *I* had graduated from there thirty-two years previously, in exactly the same spot, give or take a few square yards owing to the old school having been destroyed in a fire and then rebuilt.

Those recent graduates—all thirteen of them, sitting on the stage behind me as I spoke—listened attentively, as did most of the town, sitting quietly in the auditorium. Not one of them had come down there to see how little Ronnie Rozelle had turned out, I assure you. Everybody was there for those thirteen kids. Some of the people in the crowd hadn't had a child in school in ages. But they were there. The place was packed; it was a real community event.

The graduates told stories about each other, and you could have heard a pin drop in that big room when they spoke. At the end of the ceremony everybody rose to their feet and sang the school song, the words of which everyone knew by heart. Even me.

The thirteen honored students held each other's hands tightly while they sang it. And most of them were crying. As were many in the crowd. When it was all over, the kids hugged each other and cried some more and it was obvious that they didn't want it to end. Outside, in the warm May night, most of the town stood in the schoolyard and visited and they, too, were reluctant to go home.

So, which ceremony was the most meaningful, in the long run?

Both accomplished the same purpose. But the memory of those kids standing—hand in hand, with tears in their eyes— before the community that raised them, and stood in quiet respect before them, will be with me always.

What I experienced tonight will escape quickly.

And good riddance.

Coffee

The odds are pretty good, I'll wager, that a majority of you dozen or so people who read this weekly offering are, at this moment, either holding a cup of coffee or are in close proximity to one.

By the time I read it, I've had a couple of cups already. And, yes, I do read this stuff every Sunday morning, looking for mistakes. Which is a fruitless venture, I realize, since by then there's nothing to be done about them, sort of like the captain of the Titanic charting a course as the bow slips under. But when mistakes do pop up, coffee helps.

Coffee, in fact, helps in almost every situation.

I couldn't begin to remember even a fraction of the times—good, bad, and indifferent—when a cup of coffee wasn't my copilot. And to those of you who are ready to lecture me now regarding the unhealthy effects of too much of it, let me say only this: thanks for your interest, but don't waste your time. I am a hopeless cause, a dark disciple of Juan Valdez; there's no more chance of me giving up coffee than there is of Rosie O'Donnell and Donald Trump burying the hatchet, and not in each other.

My crack research team—Google.com—came up with a little history of this fuel that keeps me going. It seems an ancient shepherd in Caffa, Ethiopia, noticed that his sheep got perkier when they ate the red berries of a particular plant and that, when he ground them up—the berries, not the sheep—in animal fat and ate it, he felt perkier, too. I am indebted to that guy, though I am thankful that the animal fat recipe didn't catch on.

Ottoman Turks sent coffee beans out on the trade routes that crisscrossed Europe in the 1300s and, when it finally reached our neck of the woods, coffee replaced beer as New York City's favorite breakfast drink in 1668. Which may or may not be impressive to you, dependent upon where you stand on beer.

In 1773, the Boston Tea Party made the consumption of coffee an American patriotic duty and, in 1900, the Hills Brothers began canning ground coffee in vacuum tins. And the rest, as they say, . . .

Now, when it comes to a cup of joe, I'm darned particular. It can't be too weak, like the flavored water that novices sometimes brew; nor can it be overly strong, like Chester used to make on *Gunsmoke* and my brother-in-law still does in McKinney. I'm just as finicky about the vessel it is served in. I'm opposed to waxy paper cups. And, if it is a mug, it has to be a thick one. My favorite is of the hefty ceramic variety, with a thick handle. And it brightens my mood considerably to be served a cup of coffee in a diner or restaurant in a real cup with a saucer. Which used to happen all the time and now hardly ever happens at all. Ours has become a world of Styrofoam and plastic, and it's one more indication of society's slippage into darkness, in my opinion, when a fellow can't get a cup of coffee in a real cup.

There's a scene in Arthur Miller's play *A View from the Bridge* where the housewife of a dockworker tells him that the aroma of coffee being unloaded from a Brazilian ship had made all of Brooklyn thirsty for a cup all day. Her husband's response is wonderful: "That's one time, boy, to be a longshoreman is a pleasure. I could work coffee ships twenty hours a day. You go down in the hold, y'know? It's like flowers, that smell."

And he was right. There are very few fragrances as immediately identifiable or as enticing as that of coffee. My Aunt Fernie used to say that if it tasted as good as it smelled, we'd all be paupers.

The problem is that, for me at least, it does taste as good as it smells. And given the overall status of my finances, Aunt Fernie must have been on to something.

But—what the heck?—it's only money. So I'm going to have another cup. You do, too.

Father's Day,
fatherhood,
and pancakes

Today being what it is, we'll take up the subject of fathers: good, bad, and indifferent. I hope yours falls—or fell—decidedly into that first category. Mine did.

He remains a particularly bright star to steer by, fifteen years after his death and a month shy of his 101st birthday. He had the respect and affection of several generations of students in the little town where he was a teacher, coach, and superintendent for half a century, was a combat veteran of World War II, a good provider for his family, a cultivator and loyal maintainer of friendships, and he made the best pancakes I've ever tasted. Not long before he slipped away into the cruel shadowland of Alzheimer's disease, he finally told me his secret regarding those pancakes; he used Sprite instead of water in the batter.

He touched countless lives, and left the world a little better off than he found it. Which is a fine reckoning, don't you think?

Not that he was a saint, you understand. He could be moody, but not very often. And he pinched pennies a little tighter than my sisters and I would have liked when we were growing up. We never wanted for anything that we really needed but were of the shared opinion that real Cokes and Dr Peppers would have been preferable to their Safeway brand equivalents, and real ice cream would have definitely been better than mellorine, an unfortunate concoction of the '50s and '60s that seems to have since vanished completely. And thank God.

Then, when we were grown, he became generosity personified. When I married and got—in addition to a beautiful bride—three little girls and an old cat in the bargain, he stuffed nice wads of cash into their Christmas and birthday cards (except for the cat, who never got a penny). My father didn't consider my newfound brood as anything other than his grandchildren, as completely as if they were of his own bloodline.

Although he certainly saw the value of sound financial management—remember that mellorine—he never saw money as the most important thing in life, or even close to it. Which is always a convenient philosophy for a school teacher and, to my way of thinking, an admirable one for anyone.

When my sisters and I talk about him, it's never about the cash he loved to dole out for special occasions or the inheritance he left to us. It's always about the things he did and said, the example he set, and the way he smiled and his eyes lit up when we went to see him.

I'm not so stupid as to believe that everyone was as fortunate in the paterfamilias department as I was. As is the case in any other office or profession, there are fathers aplenty out there who just aren't up to the task.

Too many fellows frown and carp about it, begrudging the honor given them. And too many abdicate the responsibility altogether, leaving the mother to do all the tending and providing. That purely financial consideration is one thing—and, believe me, if I ever get to be king every jerk who fails to make his child support payments will be hunted down, marched into the clink, and made to pay up—but the even greater sin, the way I see it, is the walking away from children who would benefit enormously from a good job of fathering.

Which is sometimes the hardest job in the world, but is—at the same time—both the most important and rewarding one that a man can undertake.

In *Into That Good Night*, the memoir I wrote a decade ago, I mentioned an old navy surplus clock so many times that reviewers assumed that I put it in as a symbol for my dad. I didn't; that clock is just a clock. All through my childhood I watched him wind it every morning and, when he died, I unscrewed it from his wall and affixed it to mine. So it continues to tick away through my daily existence, not unlike his good, kind heart.

Which makes it a symbol after all, I guess. And not too shabby of one, at that.

My hope is that you will feel your own father's heartbeat on this Father's Day, as dependable and sure as that old clock's quiet ticking.

It might be a hot time
in the old town
in 100 years

I read somewhere that the average temperature on a summer day at the turn of the next century might very well be 110 degrees hereabouts.

Of course, at the turn of the next century, I won't have to worry about it and—let's face it—neither will you. But, unless they will have taken to building gigantic air-conditioned domes over towns and cities, or have devised a way to manipulate mother nature, that new crop of billions of people will have to put up with some awfully balmy days for long stretches of time.

Frankly, I very much doubt that those future generations will have made any enormous advances in making the weather behave the way they want it to. One unalterable fact common to all centuries is that the weather does exactly what it wants to. And, lately, it seems to want to turn up the heat.

The term "global warming" pops up everywhere these days—on the news and in the paper, even in conversations. It's one of the currently fashionable catchphrases, like "networking" and "gravitas" and "diversification."

With Al Gore at the helm—which I never quite understood, since he is not a scientist; though he did, remember, claim to have invented the Internet, so that might lend weight to his credentials—the global warming drum beaters are in agreement that we're in for it in the roasting department. Which is not a difficult position to support, since daily temperatures have been recorded for hundreds of years. Where their unity starts to unravel like a nylon rope is about what needs to be done to slow down the elevating temps.

I certainly won't offer any suggestions about what to do about it. I very rarely get to control the temperature in my own house, much less the entire planet. And, unlike Al Gore, I am not a scientist and have never invented a single thing.

But I do agree that summers seem to be warmer than they used to be, and winters, too. Never mind why, but when I was a boy I used to spend a good bit of my time listening to old men in my little hometown hold forth in public places. And one of their favorite topics was the bitterly frigid winters of their youths. I'd lean against a post in Bobby Stroud's hardware store or hover over a cold bottle of Grape-ette at Laurene's Café and attend my first lessons in storytelling, as those men recounted long-ago snowfalls and blue northers more indigenous to New England than East Texas. Of course, memory is oftentimes a liar, and those fellows probably weren't opposed to stretching things a bit to make their yarns better, like adding a few dashes of seasoning into a soup pot.

I don't recall them ever talking about how the summers of their boyhoods were any hotter, just how the winters were colder. So there must be something to this gradual progression of warmer climes. In just the half century that I've been paying attention—a miniscule drop in the bucket when compared to the long, straight thread of human existence—I've noticed it myself.

I'm not talking about vast glaciers melting and sending tidal waves crashing south, or even the gradual, year-by-year invasion of the expanding oceans, chewing up shorelines and bulkheads. I'm just referring to the simple fact that the winters that I recall from my childhood seemed colder than current ones, and the summers not so stifling hot. Of course, I moved down to the Gulf Coast since then, which accounts for a great deal, and—if truth be known—I'm not all that different than those old boys I used to listen to in the hardware store and the café. My memory tends to stretch things to advantage on occasion.

Anyway, I'm no Al Gore, so I don't really know what I can do about global warming. But in an effort to at least do something, I'll try not to fire up my barbecue pit too many times during July and August. The official reason being to avoid emitting thermal and harmful toxins into the atmosphere. The real reason being— you might have already guessed—that it's just too darned hot to tend to a fire.

The Fourth of July

This Wednesday, this little snippet of a song will wander through my mind: "Firecrackers poppin', lighting up the sky; hail to the flag, it's the Fourth of July."

It's from an old record album I bought in the PX of the army base I was stationed at in Illesheim, Germany in 1973. The composer and singer was Roger Miller, the King of the Road himself, and the title of the album was *Dear Folks, Sorry I Haven't Written Lately*.

I still have that record, stored away in a trunk with maybe two hundred others that I can't listen to any more because I no longer own a record player. I truly miss those big platters of wax and take them out on occasion just to look at their covers; I even miss the crackling sound that always came when the needle sank down into the grooves. I'm of a generation that still refers — to the confusion of any young people in earshot — to a place where CDs can be purchased as a "record store."

That Roger Miller LP must have contained other good tunes, but the one that got caught in my brain and is still there was the short, simple ditty about Independence Day.

I guess that's because it's basically a simple holiday. Coming, as it does, in the hottest part of the year, it's given over pretty much to picnics and fireworks and outdoor concerts. There's no telling how many hotdogs and hamburgers will be gobbled down this Wednesday, washed down with considerable tonnage of soft drinks and beer.

Amid all that hoopla and food and drink a little patriotism works its way in, chiefly of the flag-waving variety. Probably the closest we've come to a commemoration worthy of the event was in 1976, the Bicentennial, which—as those of you who remember it will probably agree—was one heck of a party. What with church bells tolling, the Hudson River full of hundreds of tall ships, and the world's great orchestras blaring out "Yankee Doodle Dandy" and "The Stars and Stripes Forever."

That year we actually reflected, I think, on the handful of men who put their lives on the line one hot summer night in Philadelphia and transformed themselves into both traitors and patriots with the stoke of a pen.

Eleven years later, the crafters of the Constitution emerged exhausted from the same building, having sufficiently corralled their strong wills—though not quite tightly enough, leaving the abolition of slavery out of their factoring—into a single document that would become the new nation's bedrock and backbone. That night, somebody called out to Benjamin Franklin, asking him "Well, Doctor, what did we get—a Republic or a Monarchy?" The old man—weary, weak, and deciding whether sleep or a drink should come first—responded with seven words which found their way into history: "A Republic, if you can keep it."

We've somehow managed, amid wars and tragedies and political bickering, to keep it.

I've never been to Independence Hall. The only time I was ever in Philadelphia was when I flew in there on my way to Fort Dix, New Jersey, where I would be shipped out to Germany, where I bought that Roger Miller record that I can't listen to anymore.

But I will go there; it's on my agenda. I will stand in that old building and in the very room that is—by any measure—the birthplace of the United States. Because, like most folks, I tend to take what happened there in 1776 and 1787 for granted, and lose the pure glory and bravery of it in my everyday life.

This Wednesday, that little snippet of a song will pop up in my mind, just like it does every year. "Firecrackers poppin', lighting up the sky; hail to the flag, it's the Fourth of July." And it's fitting, I think, that it is simplicity itself. Because there's not really anything so very complicated about loving your country and celebrating its founding.

You have yourself a fine Independence Day. Eat more hot dogs than you ought to and wave a flag. It's your right, and your heritage. And maybe spare a minute or two to remember the event that bought it for you.

The shade of trees

It's a Tuesday morning, and I'm settled comfortably in a chair in the shade of a pecan tree in the back yard. The television weatherman said it would be awfully humid today, and for once he was absolutely right. It's so clammy, in fact, that it seems altogether possible to reach up and wring liquid right out of the air, like twisting a wet washrag.

I've mown half of the yard and am considering mowing the other half. Two things might keep me from it for a while (other than the aforementioned humidity and its attendant blistering heat). First, the lawnmower currently in my employ is the cheapest model available. I used to have a big riding mower, but it took to dying in stages, its major organs shutting down one after another, requiring expensive transplants. After several years of shelling out cash to keep it alive, I finally pulled the plug and decided to go back to the basics, as it were, and got myself a little rig that isn't even self-propelled. Sound economy, I figured, and a darned good workout to boot.

It seemed like a good idea at the time.

But this morning the prospect of pushing that little devil through high grass and soggy air will likely keep me in this chair for quite a while. The second deterrent is that this tree, which produces pitiful excuses for pecans, does provide glorious shade.

I suppose people have been relaxing in the shade of trees for as long as there have been trees and people. Long before prehistoric humans discovered fire, crafted the first wheel, or perceived the advantages of opposable thumbs, one bright soul must have wandered into the shade of a tree and thought: "Ah, now that's better."

And how right he or she was. Like right now, not a good spit from where I'm sitting sunlight is blaring down, but under this tree it's several degrees cooler and when a little breeze wanders into the yard it's downright refreshing. Out there, the same breeze would feel like the blast of a furnace.

I don't see how folks can live in places without trees. It's a matter of personal preference, of course, but a desert just doesn't do much for me at all. Unless, that is, I happen to be looking at it from under a tree, the barren, rocky landscape framed by low branches and dark, cool shade.

Even in the middle of urban sprawl, shady places offer tranquil havens. I'm thinking of the plaza in front of the Wortham Theater in Houston, and of tiny Grammercy Park in Manhattan, beside a hotel I stayed in once. In those places, all the clamor and honking and stress of a big city is out there in abundance among the steel and concrete, but those shady arbors offer sanctuaries where you can sit on a bench, take a deep breath, and watch the splotchy, dark shadows on the ground as they mingle with yellow medallions of sunlight that have dropped down through the branches.

Shade is the simplest of blessings, of course. But it is a blessing, nonetheless.

The long-gone poet Joyce Kilmer came up with these lines that many of us had to memorize and then regurgitate in elementary school: "Poems are made by fools like me, but only God can make a tree."

Personally, I believe that. And I'm grateful that He (God, not Mr. Kilmer—who was a male, by the way, who was either named after a particular relative or family friend or had parents with a wicked sense of humor) had the creation of trees on His agenda. I'm just as grateful for their soothing byproduct.

Now, if you'll excuse me, the little mower is grinning at me, so I think I'll go ahead and crank it up and finish the job. Then, after a shower, I might just come back out here to the shade of this tree and either plop back down in this chair or stretch out in the hammock. I'll bring whatever paperback mystery yarn I'm currently reading, or I'll drag along the mammoth biography of the British author W. Somerset Maugham that I'm determined to finish, a chore proving to be not unlike pushing that mower through high grass.

Old news

Owing to the fact that I am a certifiable packrat, I have a big plastic crate containing enough old newspaper pages to represent a small glade of sacrificed timber. Every time I see something in the morning paper that I deem worth saving, it goes into the crate. And now the archives are bulging to the extent that I will soon have to invest in a second container.

The papers aren't in chronological order, and I followed no criteria regarding their selection beyond my having considered them important and/or interesting.

Let's take a look.

Here's the front page of the *Houston Chronicle* for Wednesday, August 31, 2005, with a one word headline a couple of inches tall: HEARTBREAKING. Beneath it is an aerial photograph of New Orleans, flooded after Hurricane Katrina. And here's the *New York Times* from less than a month later showing bumper to bumper traffic inching its way north fleeing Rita. My wife and I—along with our four cats—were in that traffic, which turned out to be the largest mass evacuation in American history.

This big headline on the February 2, 2003, issue of the *Brazosport Facts* says COLUMBIA IS LOST. The photo above it is one of those images that became immediately ingrained in our national memory banks: bits of the shuttle soaring back into the atmosphere over East Texas, streaking the perfectly blue sky with trails of white.

Famous people's obituaries comprise a respectable chunk of my collection. Let's see now, here's John Connally (1993), Anwar Sadat (1981), Barbara Jordan (1996), Jimmy Stewart (1997), and John Wayne (1979). There're lots of these, probably forty or fifty notices of famous folks' deaths. Here's Jackie Kennedy and Richard Nixon within a month of each other in 1994; talk about the two ends of the political spectrum finally finding common ground.

The big departures—the ones that stopped us cold for a few days—are all here too, all the way back to six front pages about President Kennedy's assassination and funeral. My mother was responsible for me having these; she was a packrat, too. And here are pages for Ronald Reagan, Princess Diana, and Pope John Paul II.

Here's a big color photo of the opening ceremonies of the 1984 Summer Olympic Games in Los Angeles, and here's Chris Burke galloping around the bases on the *Chronicle's* front page for Monday, October 10, 2005. The headline is A GAME FOR THE AGES: ASTROS 7, BRAVES 6, 18 INNINGS. That was baseball's longest postseason game ever, and it kept me glued to the television for nearly six hours.

The lead story in the Lifestyle & Entertainment section for Thursday, May 14, 1998, is called "A lotta yada yada yada about nada" and is about the final episode of "Seinfeld" which aired that night. I wish I had something about the last episode of "MASH", but I wasn't as diligent that day as I should have been, and nothing went into the crate.

War is well-represented here, with the various conflicts of the various Presidents Bush. And here's the invasion of Granada, which always sounded more like the title of an opera to me than a war.

Here's the very last issue of the *Houston Post*. It plopped into my driveway on the morning of Tuesday, April 18, 1995, and I didn't know till I watched the news that night that its long run—well over a century—was over.

The *Wall Street Journal* used to call itself the "daily diary of the American dream." I fully realize that some ad man dreamed that up to sell more subscriptions, but I liked it. In fact, I see the whole meaning of newspapers as being the daily diary of our daily experience. And my big crate of yellowing pages is a small parcel of that total experience that I can look back through occasionally.

It just seems to me that hanging on to scraps of current events—little bits of proof that we were here and were about our business—ought to be important.

Whoever inherits this crate—when my obituary pops up one of these days in the pages of the morning paper—might just find it interesting that on Saturday, December 18, 1982, one of the programs listed in the eleven channels of the television guide was *The Lawrence Welk Show,* or that jogging suits were 20 percent off at Brown's Department Store in Freeport.

Of course, the recipient of all these pages might just put them out by the curb for recycling. It'll be their call.

Sibling rivalry and resolution

Today is my sister Janie's birthday, which she will celebrate by sailing past the Statue of Liberty early this morning into New York harbor after a cruise to Bermuda. She won't see this column until she gets home, unless they have taken to selling this paper alongside the *New York Times* in Manhattan. Which they certainly should, but in all likelihood don't.

I actually owe Janie an apology, and the anniversary of her birth is a good time to deliver it. When I wrote *Into that Good Night*, a memoir about my father, his Alzheimer's ordeal, and the little town he and my mother raised us in, I cast Janie in a pretty bad light in the early chapters. In fact, she came off as a moody, self-centered, rude little thing. She *was* these things, you understand, at least in regards to me. She was a young teenager in the very early 1960s, all Sandra Dee-ish in bobby socks, ponytail, and pleated skirt. Janie is five years older than me and, when a brother and sister are nine and fourteen, those five years constitute one heck of a wide gulf.

I did a constant tap dance on her nerves, to put it mildly.

So, while I was altogether truthful when describing her behavior towards yours truly in those chapters, I really should have checked with her before putting it all in. Or, at least, I probably should have given her a little warning, so that she wouldn't have seen all that description for the first time when I sent her a copy of the bound galley proofs.

I teach my writing students that every story better have a little—or a lot—of irony. So here it is for this tale: Janie's and my relationship eventually grew into a deep friendship that no one would have predicted in those ancient days when the highlight of my week was watching *Have Gun, Will Travel* on television and hers was watching *American Bandstand.*

Hardly a day goes by that we don't talk to each other on the phone and when we get together we stay up late into the night yakking. She and our older sister Diane—who married when I was five and moved into her own house, leaving the stage, or the battleground, to Janie and me—are two of the great constants in my life, dependable and enduring. All in all, I'm very lucky in the sister department—I was the baby, and the only boy—and it makes me sad that many adult siblings don't have the close bond that we do.

This morning, Janie and her traveling companions intend to go from their ship up to Amsterdam Avenue for breakfast at Sarabeth's, the restaurant that my wife Karen and I recommended years ago and that she visits whenever she's in New York. She'll have the oatmeal pancakes, her favorite. Then she'll fly home to her husband of over forty years, to her children and grandchildren, and to a happy, productive life.

She told me, on her last trip down to visit us, that she has made a list of four goals that she calls her "out of the box" intentions. From least important to most, she wants to: 1) fly in a hot-air balloon, 2) take a parachute jump (attached to someone who knows considerably more about it than she does), 3) go on a camera safari on the Serengeti, and 4) work for a month or two as a volunteer in an orphanage in Africa, even if the most that she can do is hold the babies and rock them.

That last one pretty much sums up the woman that that long-ago teenager became.

Happy birthday, Janie. I hereby publicly apologize for being a pain when I was a little boy and for writing about how much of one I thought you were. I apologize for the time that I read portions of that book to your students in the elementary school where you were a teacher, causing them to snicker and point at you. No, I take that one back; it was great fun and you thought so, too.

And I thank you for the long years of our close friendship, which might be an "out of the box" relationship between a sister and brother. But, if so, it's a box that I am happily out of.

A new leaf
in khaki tan

This Thursday—August 2—will mark the thirty-fifth anniversary
of my raising my hand and repeating the oath that delivered me
into the United States Army. It's a date that has stuck in my mind,
and every August 2 I think of it. In other words, that date is a legit-
imate milestone.

My trusty Funk & Wagnalls desk dictionary defines a milestone as either "a post or marker set up to indicate mileage from
a given point" or "an important event or turning point." Let's go
with the second one this morning, and leave the mileage business for another day, even though there was considerable of it
over those thirty-five years.

Whether or not my taking that oath was important is debat-
able—I served most of my stint working as a clerk in an office and
enjoying schnitzel and other Bavarian delights; the closest I came
to keeping America safe was standing long, cold stints of guard
duty in a parking lot full of surplus jeep trailers that nobody had
any interest in stealing—but it was most definitely a turning
point. In fact, those two years turned me around completely.

When Uncle Sam sent his greetings in 1972 I was very much
involved in what I called my "figuring things out" phase. I had
been to college—for all of five weeks—having stayed at Sam
Houston University only long enough to convince myself, and
my academic advisor, that I had no more interest in attending
classes than a pig had in dancing a polka. So I turned back up at

my parents' house and spent a year and a half working at Gibson's Discount Center, reading one novel after another, and running around with my old high school chums. In that place and time, "running around" meant driving along country roads drinking beer obtained from bootleggers and hoping that some girls were in the vicinity and that county deputies were not.

My "figuring things out" phase came to an abrupt halt when the Selective Service System figured they needed my services for a couple of years. So, I was swept off to Dallas to take that oath, then to Fort Ord, California, for basic training and clerk–typist school, then to Germany where I was a job order clerk in a maintenance repair shop and a diligent guardian of decommissioned trailers.

When I mustered out, I got down to business and finished my degree at Sam Houston in less than three years, took a job at the school in East Texas where I did my practice teaching, and have been a high school teacher ever since.

I've taught senior English for a long time now, and I encourage my students to skip the "figuring things out" phase and get on with a better plan. I'm awfully careful not to make any suggestions regarding military service. But when a student tells me he or she is considering enlisting, I tell them what my stint did for me.

But I do remind them that the big difference now is, of course, that we are at war. When I got drafted, the Vietnam conflict was in its final death throes, and President Nixon was closing up shop in that part of the world. So I was allowed to enlist with Tim Stroud, a friend from home, on the buddy plan for basic training. We even got to request our permanent postings; Hawaii for Tim and Germany for me. I was never in harm's way during my enlistment, unless you count the chance of getting a chill on those frigid nights of guard duty. It's true that I had to put my life on hold for a couple of years but—let's face it—the "figuring things out" thing just wasn't working, and I needed a jump start. Make no mistake about it: it was those two years in the service that instilled the confidence, the discipline, and the determination that put me on the right track.

Some of my former students are in Iraq right now. And I hope that soon they'll all be safely home.

What I really hope is that someday—say thirty-five years from now—they will realize that their time in uniform made a real difference, both in the country they served and in themselves, as well.

Culinary perfection
among magnolias and
mint juleps

Have you ever had a perfect dining experience? I'm talking about an ideal marriage of place, ambiance, service, and food; a phenomenal breaking of bread that sent you very nearly floating away from it in satisfied bliss. Have you ever had one of those?

I have. And it was just a couple of weeks ago, in Vicksburg, Mississippi.

Actually, I've enjoyed several excellent dinners in that little city. Almost twenty years ago I had a Gulf flounder stuffed with shrimp and crabmeat that would rate pretty high on anyone's list. Then on the very night before the one I'm about to tell you about, my wife Karen and I ate a fine meal in a fancy Italian place on Washington Street, concluding with a tiramisu that could become habit-forming.

But the next night—ahh, the next night. That's when I scored a personal best in dining experiences. Here's the recipe, in case you want to replicate it:

First, eat a particularly disappointing lunch. In Vicksburg, you can accomplish that at a little place with a placard outside that advertises "The Best Sandwiches in Town." If that is indeed the case then Vicksburg suffers greatly when it comes to sandwiches. My Reuben was a pasty, tasteless conglomeration mashed between two slices of wheat bread. That's right; wheat bread. Karen's chili dog was nothing more special than a wiener in a dry bun with a glob of canned chili—all of it zapped for a few seconds in a microwave. The Reuben was called the Morgan Freeman and the dog was the Andy Griffith. And those two admirable fellows should sue that shop; they've been publicly disgraced.

Next, spend a relaxing afternoon touring a couple of antebellum era houses, climbing steep, creaking staircases and looking at sundry chamber pots and plate warmers and crystal flycatchers.

Then, after a short nap at your hotel, get yourself over to the Anchuca Mansion on East First Street, so steeped in history that it's in the National Register of Historic Places. Built in 1830 by a cotton magnate, it was used as a hospital during General Grant's siege of the city in the Civil War, and President of the Confederacy Jefferson Davis made one of his last speeches from the wrought-iron balcony between majestic while columns on the front porch. Now it's a highly acclaimed bed and breakfast inn and restaurant.

Your first stop should be the library bar, which is more like the comfortable den of an avid reader than a tavern. There are no tables or booths, just overstuffed chairs and an inviting old sofa. The walls are all well-stocked bookshelves and handsomely framed prints. The bartender, Beau, is more like a host who's invited you over for dinner than an employee; he's friendly, chatty, and very, very good at his craft.

Spend a while in that room; let the long history of the place settle around you. Let the various ghosts move though. Then, with one of Beau's frosty creations in hand, wander into the dining room. The tables are covered in white linen with fresh-cut roses in bowls; late afternoon sunlight streams through windows that look out on a carefully manicured garden bordered with crape myrtles blooming more profusely than the ones in my yard back home.

Let the white-jacketed waiter tell you about the menu items, then choose the house salad in a tart poppy seed dressing, followed by chicken roasted in lemon and herbs, peppery and crackling crisp on the outside, tender and buttery inside. The supporting players are steamed vegetables bathed in a chardonnay marinade and a darned-near amazing creation where wild rice and orzo pasta cavort with pineapple, raisins, cranberries, nuts, peppers and onions. Have it all with a bottle of Pinot Grigio.

Then oscillate for a minute or two between the Anchuca Bonzo cake and the maple bourbon pecan pie. We opted for the cake, a multi-layered business involving dark chocolate mocha ganache, amaretto mascarpone, cream cheese, whipped cream, and caramel. Bring matters to a close with a cup of strong chicory coffee.

Now, stroll between the carriage house and the mansion proper along a brick path under majestic magnolias to your car, drive out to one of the scenic overlooks high up on the old town's bluffs, click your *Showboat* soundtrack to "Old Man River," snuggle up close to your significant other, and watch the wide Mississippi move slowly along, the last silver light of the day dancing on its swirling surface.

So, there's my perfect dining experience. What's yours?

Cheap books

Let me begin by admitting, right up front, to being unashamedly and unrepentantly on the lookout for cheap books. More accurately, I am constantly in the market for good books at cheap prices. Some of the best treasures on my shelves came from clearance tables at bookstores, from garage sales, and from a discount mail order outfit in Connecticut.

At garage sales, I've dug my way through many a pile of books on card tables or in paper boxes, like a prospector sifting through an acre or so of river sand looking for a speck of gold.

The end result of all of this is that I have what many people would consider too many books. Of course, some people would consider any at all too many, so I can't spend any time worrying about that.

But when my shelves start groaning, I weed some volumes out and either donate them to charity sales or haul them off to a second-hand store to sell them, because I could no more throw a book away than I could toss a puppy out into a blizzard. Recently, I made a grand total of twenty bucks for three full boxes of hardbacks. Which amounted to a profit of about a nickel per book, hardly enough to cover the cost—these days—of the gasoline it took to lug them up to Houston.

But that's okay. Most of those books will be read again, and then, probably, again. And that's what books are for. I know people who have books on their shelves as decoration only, placed there because of their handsome leather bindings or because the covers blend into the color scheme of the room. Once, I naturally gravitated toward someone's bookshelves and found a row of perfectly new, obviously unopened French texts. Since I knew that my hosts neither spoke nor read French, I realized that the books were purely cosmetic, like props on a stage set.

That's fine with me. But the numerous books in my house are both keepsakes and reference tools. Though perhaps not enhancing the ambiance of the decor, they're pulled down on occasion to be thumbed through, read or re-read, and actually used.

Step over here to the bookcase and let me show you.

That little one right there, with the worn cloth binding, is *The Yellow Room* by Mary Roberts Rinehart; it was the first mystery novel I ever read, and the catalyst for a lifetime of pleasure. I've read those novels by Gore Vidal—the seven big ones there together, all of them set in Washington, DC, from the Revolutionary War through World War II—twice each, and may or may not read them again. But there they are, just in case. That covey of poetry anthologies is for when a snippet of verse pecks at my brain, or I have a decision to make and need to read Frost's "The Road Not Taken" to nudge me. And *Kristin Lavransdatter* by Sigrid Undset, in those three volumes there at the end, may never get read at all. Who knows? Maybe sometime in my future dotage a long Scandinavian saga might be just the ticket for a couple of weeks one blustery winter.

I got that boxed set for one dollar at a garage sale years ago. That same day I found an early Anne Sexton. Not a first edition, but not bad for fifty cents.

There's another reason I'm all in favor of buying books on the cheap, and it might sound silly to you. As the author of six books—all of which are sometimes found on discount racks and clearance carts—I like to imagine a shopper unknown to me—

maybe in Duluth or Peoria or Tallahassee—on a crisp Saturday morning lifting up one of my efforts, thumbing through it, reading the first couple of paragraphs, paying their two dollars, and taking it home. Where it might just provide them with an acceptable few hours of reading and maybe end up in their bookcase. Or, better yet, passed along to a friend to read.

It's wishful thinking, I know. But, after all, what's wrong with a little of that? It's a nice feeling, the possibility that some of my books are wandering around out there in the wide world, making their hopeful way like Dickens' pitiful waifs, finding refuge, finally, on a friendly shelf or bedside table.

By the way, the twenty dollars that I made at the used bookstore never left the building. A handsome copy of Derek Walcott's poems called out to me, and three paperback whodunits.

The bill came to $24.95.

For the crude, rude, and mean, let the games begin

I see where they've had themselves something called the Texas Redneck Games up near Athens. I guess the location is owing to the fact that Athens, Greece, was the birthplace of the Olympics, and the association was obvious even to the creators of such a festival as this one.

According to Henderson County officials—who want any such future shenanigans outlawed—it was a four-day melee of "nudity, rowdiness, intoxication, people running wild on four-wheelers . . . underage drinking, fights and assaults." Sounds like great fun, don't you think? And proof positive that we've hit a low-water mark in the whole civilized society thing.

So now that we have an open-air gathering where the only agenda is mass participation in obnoxious behavior, why not go whole hog and plan a whole season of contests revolving around crude conduct? I guarantee you folks will flock to them in droves, and the television networks will love it; they'll have sufficient fodder for reality programs to fill up every minute of their airtime.

First up in the season should be the Racism Rally, where prejudiced people go head to head armed only with their hatred of each other. One of the stellar events would be the N-word sprints, where contestants have to use that word as many times as possible in complete sentences (adherence to grammatical rules won't be required) in a three-minute period. Another event will be the Big Bigot But Bout, where the contender must begin with "I'm not prejudiced, but …" and conclude with a completely prejudiced statement or joke. The racial joke shoot-out will probably be a great crowd-pleaser, as well.

Next on the tour will be the Hypocrisy Hoopla. Here, upstanding citizens will simply judge each other in all manners of situations. Each must present what they consider to be valid credentials—be they scriptural, doctrinal or just plain snobbery. An event called Class Clash—commonly referred to as the "Our Sort of People" brawl—will be big in this competition, pitting various strata of society against each other. And who won't enjoy the "Don't Walk the Walk" Scramble? Watching people who profess to be one thing but whose actions prove them to be something else is always amusing.

Then there will be the Pessimism Party, where folks will be provided any number of opportunities to be downright negative. Surely the most popular event will be the Dishing Dash, where contestants will be given the names of people and will have to respond, rapid fire, with as many negative things about each person as they can come up with. And, in the Glass Half Empty challenge, they will be required to give every negative slant on several hypothetical situations.

Next up will be the Meanness Marathon. There will be two divisions here: criminals and just basically mean people. The criminals will compete in Armed Robbery, Breaking and Entering, Mugging, Phone Scams, Credit Card Theft and Physical Abuse. Just basically mean people will have events like Surliness, Road Rage, Saying Vulgar Things in Public, Blowing Off Child Support Payments and Verbal Abuse. There is a youth category in the Meanness Marathon, so that children can compete in the areas of bullying, ridicule and general assault.

The regular season will conclude with the ever-popular Gossip Games. One of the matches will be the Confidential Contest, where the participant must say "Just between you and me ..." and then blurt out everything he knows all over the place like a town crier. And don't forget the Stretch Match, where events must be stretched out to the most degrading, harmful and hurtful contortion possible, and factual accuracy must be wandered away from as quickly and effectively as possible.

Finally, the Grand Champion will be determined in a Super Bowl, where the winners of each contest will go at each other head-on, employing their unique weapons to full advantage.

But the winner of the Hypocrisy Hoopla won't participate in the Super Bowl. He or she will be the judge, since they're so good at that.

Mr. Chaucer in the fall;
Mrs. Browning in the spring

Tomorrow, I'll begin my thirty-first year as a public school employee, most of them as a teacher of senior English. And I've come to depend on what we do in class to provide the perennial landmarks by which my students and I navigate the seasons toward their graduation and my next summer break. Commendable goals, both, in my opinion.

I love teaching that course to seniors. Because by the time they get to me, the all-holy TAKS test is in their past, and the great wide world that they are chomping at the bit to get into is in their very near future. It's a fine time to traverse a smorgasbord of literary offerings that they don't figure—at the outset—will be their cup of tea. But which most of them come around to liking just fine.

I stick very close to the tried and true curriculum for English IV that hasn't changed much since I was a senior, or long before that. It's a chronological survey of British literature, from Anglo-Saxon times to the present, covering a good bit of English history along the way.

We always start with *Beowulf*. Drunken soldiers being ripped apart and eaten by a monster is a great icebreaker and gets the kids' attention right off the bat. Then, about the time that the leaves start to change in other places where they actually have autumn, we fall into step with Chaucer's pilgrims in *The Canterbury Tales*. Sometime between Halloween and Thanksgiving, we'll plod like ducks down to the library for a few days to dig up the goods for a big research paper. Then, as a last bit of business before the winter break, it's on to a long bout with Mr. Shakespeare.

This week when that new class looks at the printed syllabus I'll give them and sees that the entire third six weeks unit is devoted to *Hamlet,* more than a few students will cringe. Or moan. Or feel a little sick. But I'll wager that by the time we finish that play—having read every syllable of it out loud, with students taking turns reading the characters' lines (except for King Claudius, which is reserved each year for yours truly)—most of them will have found a lot in it to ponder. It is the great favorite of most of the kids, year after year.

We begin the second semester in the dead of winter. First off we'll enter some deep, dark forests, wandering through selected bits of *Paradise Lost, Pilgrim's Progress* and *Gulliver's Travels,* which a National Merit Scholar finalist a few years ago, probably groggy while burning the midnight oil, referred to in an essay as *Gilligan's Island.*

Springtime brings us into a wide sun-splashed field of poetry, from the seventeenth century through the Romantics and the Victorians. Finally we dip into a little Dylan Thomas and John Keats and end up with *Lord of the Flies,* a novel.

Now, you might wonder just what this nine-month immersion into the history and literature of England is likely to do for a high school graduate. Certainly those seniors will wonder, when they look at the bill of fare on the first day.

Here's my response. First, they will—at the end of it—have the basic literary foundation that college-bound students will be expected to have. Second, whether they are off to college or not, they will have tromped around in new intellectual territory, and discussed and written about what they found there. And third, they might just stumble on some truths along the way, and the beautifully crafted language that conveys them.

And those truths might just come in handy along life's journey. Here are two cases in point.

A former student told me once that he faced a horrible setback early in his career. He went on to say that part of what motivated him to pick himself up and build his life back was a snippet he remembered from Tennyson's poem "Ulysses," that told him "to strive, to seek, to find, and not to yield."

Finally, here's how some of the material that we'll start this week once came in handy for me. When I stood by my father's coffin just before it was lowered into the ground, any number of phrases or platitudes could have come to mind. But it was Horatio's brief farewell to the slain Hamlet—"Good night, sweet prince, and flights of angels sing thee to thy rest"—that I whispered into that cold November afternoon.

It's a good road that we travel in that class, and I look forward to another trip down it.

You're only as old
as the magazines
you take

My first copy of the AARP magazine just came in the mail, and that's something of a milestone, I guess.

Actually, I could have joined the American Association of Retired Persons five years ago. Not because I was retired, which I'm not, but because that's when I turned 50. Which, as many of you know, is their entry criteria, sort of like the "you must be this tall" signs that used to stand beside the scarier rides at Astroworld.

It took me this long to sign up because I just never could bring myself to enlist in a confederacy of senior citizens. I mean, come on, I realize that I've had several at-bats, but it's hardly the late innings just yet. And joining the AARP seemed like stepping into the foothills of the mountain range named Old Age. And I wasn't anywhere near ready to go there.

I wasn't ready, that is, until friends began mentioning the discounts they were getting with their AARP cards.

I mean, hanging onto one's youth is one thing, but saving a few bucks here and there is entirely another. And if that means lining up for the senior early bird special, then so be it.

So, I'm a card-carrying member now, and here is the first issue of the magazine to prove it. Let's take a look.

There's a picture of Tony Bennett on the cover standing beside Christina Aguilera, who is virtually broadcasting youth and vitality beside Mr. Bennett's silver mane and wrinkled, much-lived-in visage. The editors were going for a contrast, surely. A counterbalance; something old, something new—that sort of thing. I'm guessing there will always be somebody old on every cover. I just hope there's not a centerfold.

First off—as with any magazine that arrives—I have to gut it. Out comes all those pesky cards, some attached, some loose, and that full page of stiff paper that keeps the whole rig from having the limberness that a magazine ought to have. There are two cards pushing life insurance, one health care, another a rheumatoid arthritis treatment and several touting cruise lines and rental car outfits. Apparently American retired persons are expected to make their health and their travels high priorities.

Flipping through, I see there's a good bit in here about the best ways to manage retirement accounts, to tend gardens and create good (but healthy) things to eat and much about interesting places to visit. There's an abundance of ads for beds that mechanically lift and bend and vibrate.

Here's a plug for the *South Beach Diet* and more than a few hawking medicine for people who are either in the bathroom too often or not often enough.

One of the articles this month is titled, "Is There Life After Death?" Now there's a topic that will likely catch the attention of this particular publication's readership. More so than subscribers of, say, *Seventeen* or *Vogue*. Another piece is about a ninety-five-year-old woman who is going back to college to get her master's degree in history, a subject that she should do well at—don't you think?—having seen so much of it in person. And here's a sidebar about older people needing to be awfully careful when entering Internet chat rooms. "Here be dragons"—the author seems to be saying—among the sly, youthful predators set to pounce on us like wolves on spring lambs. Or, more accurately, on old goats.

Over all, it looks like a fine magazine, a real dandy. Seeing it in my mailbox probably won't fetch the smile that seeing

American History or *The Atlantic Monthly* gets, but it will provide a nice bit of scanning and flipping during *Sunday Night Football* and *American Idol*. And it's got a big crossword puzzle; so it passes one of my litmus tests for a useful publication.

On the last page, facing the inside of the back cover, where the best essays always appear in *The New York Times Magazine*, *Newsweek* and *Texas Monthly*, there isn't an essay at all. There's a list of famous people who turn fifty this month, all of them grinning ear to ear, as if ecstatic to have actually made it.

That page is a little depressing, since all of those people are five years younger than me. To be honest, I'd just as soon they'd put an essay there instead. Even one about acid reflux or the loss of bone density.

Not the greatest
show on earth

A few weeks ago my wife Karen and I watched a television news piece where elephants were led down out of their railway cars and marched through downtown Houston to the arena where the Ringling Brothers and Barnum & Bailey circus would be performing. At which point I fully expected Karen to say that she thought it would be a good idea for us to go to one of the shows. But she didn't, and I kept my mouth shut.

Now don't get me wrong. I like the circus and have since I went to my first one when I was seven or eight. I never considered running away to join one; my mother's three square meals a day and occasional sweet potato pie were too good to abandon. But Karen, you see, absolutely loves the circus, mainly because she has such an affinity for animals but also because of all the glitter and music and hoopla. So we've gone on occasion.

Several years ago, when our girls had moved away and we were left with only cats, we attended the Ringling Brothers show in Houston along with about a trillion screaming children and their young parents. When I went to the concession stand to buy Karen some cotton candy, a little girl in line with her mother watched me for a long while before asking if I was there with my grandchildren.

So, to use a currently popular phrase, I'm down with circuses, just not as down with them as my wife is. And the first one I ever saw rolled into Oakwood, my hometown, along about 1959 or 1960. I'm thinking it was in the fall, but I'm not sure. So I fired out a couple of emails to some old Oakwood friends and to my sister, Janie, who sent out some more. The horde of messages that I got back about that circus were conflicting, at best. It seems that everyone who remembers it at all remembers it differently, but more about that next time.

I do recall that that little troupe traveled by truck, not train, though it set up its tent in the open lot beside the railroad track where the new post office would later be built. Even that post office is gone now; Oakwood has worked its way through three post offices in my lifetime.

Anyway, about that time my parents had decided to surprise my sister Janie and me with a trip down to Houston to see the big Ringling Brothers show at the downtown Coliseum. I think my father had even agreed to spring for a room at the Rice Hotel, lavish doings from a man who encouraged my mother to re-use aluminum foil rather than buy a new roll.

Then my sister and I threw a monkey wrench in the gears. We wanted, you see, to forego that trip to the city and go with our friends to see the performance of that little circus that had come to town. Apparently the dates were conflicting, and it could be either one or the other.

Our parents tried to sway us over to the Houston trip. They were quiet, accommodating people, but once locked into a plan, they tended to want to stay the course.

But we persisted and probably whined, and we ended up going to the sorry little circus which included a couple of tired old horses, a fat little girl, in glitter-covered leotards, who rode the horses, her father who did a few rope tricks, two scraggly bears who wrestled two local fellows (who might have been any number of people who were remembered by my Oakwood contingent), and a banana-eating contest with a baboon, in which either Jerry Eldridge or his brother, Bobby, shoveled down five or six bananas while the monkey, out of the challenger's eyesight, simply held his and looked at it.

Our parents didn't go that night. And Janie and I have always known that they were disappointed in not doing the Houston trip. So, in fact, were we, if truth be known.

The televised images of those glamorous elephants a month or so ago brought back that long-ago circus in a field beside the railroad tracks in Oakwood. That little show—that had not even one elephant (of that I'm pretty certain: surely I'd remember an elephant) nor much in the way of glamour—clamped tight to my memory, as it did in many other folks. At least the general memory of it did, even if the details are fuzzy.

Old facts clashing
in the night

Recently, before reporting back to the high school where I soldier on toward that enormous state pension that I'll take them up on soon, I wanted to finish a bunch of these Sunday columns during the dog days of summer. Sort of like a farmer filling his barn up with hay before the winter sets in. At least the way farmers used to, that is, before the invention of those big rolls of hay that dot meadows now like giant pork roasts.

One of the pieces I wrote was about a tiny circus that once wandered into Oakwood, my hometown. You might have read it here in this little corner of the paper last week. And I think you would agree it was simplicity itself.

But I can report that it ignited a lively little grassfire up in Oakwood, and among folks who lived there at the time. I was a little boy when this took place, so I needed some help getting things right. I knew that show's menagerie included a bear, two underfed horses and a listless baboon that seemed always bored with whatever events were transpiring.

Somebody wrestled the bear and somebody else entered a banana-eating contest with the monkey. And I have a crystal-clear image of the head of the family that made up the troupe; he was thin as a rail and smoked one cigarette after another, even while doing the rope tricks that comprised his contribution to the program. His daughter was about my age, and there was way too much of her for the tight leotards she wore when she did some sorts of tricks on the back of those sway-backed horses. Beyond those few impressions, my mind was blank.

So I e-mailed my friends, Cathy and Carla, who would have been a year younger than me when this all went down, but who might have paid better attention. And I shot a line to my sister, Janie. Then they all e-mailed several more people each and what finally came back to me were the recollections of about fifteen folks. Few of whom remember that circus the same way, and all of whom are certain that their version is correct.

Nearly everybody agreed that it was either Jerry Eldridge or his brother, Bobby, who challenged the baboon in the banana contest. And more than a few people recalled that it was two bears, not one. Where the jury is very much still out is just who wrestled them. Leo Minter is the leading contender among those who responded, and then the field is wide open, with about six names popping up, including Jerry Eldridge again, who might have done double duty with the bear and the monkey.

Everybody agrees that the tent was where I said it was, not to be mistaken for another tent that was put up some summers out by the highway, when a roller skating rink set up shop. Sheryl Anders, my sister's friend, remembers that the little circus family went to church that Sunday at the Church of Christ, though I don't see how that skinny rope twirler managed to forego a ciga-rette for the length of a church service. And Joe Radford, Janie and Sheryl's classmate, maintains it was a medicine show and not a circus at all.

So, the end result of all this is that there was definitely a per-formance of some type that took place in a tent beside the rail-road track about 1959 or 1960. Somebody wrestled a bear—maybe two bears—and somebody was taken in by a baboon, who sat holding his banana while the opponent—whoever he was—ate several. Beyond those basic facts, everything else is pretty much up in the air. Where it is likely to stay.

Now if you think this is odd, then why don't you try dredging up some minor event from forty or fifty years ago, contact a few folks who were there at the time and are still above ground, and ask for a few details. Accounts will vary, my friend; I assure you.

What this all did, I think, was get some good people thinking about a simpler time, probably with great fondness. I seriously doubt that a circus coming into town now—even a small town—would cause very much excitement.

When someone has a hundred or so television channels to choose from, iPods to listen to, and a cell phone permanently affixed to his or her face, a mangy bear and a bored baboon aren't likely to garner much attention.

A distant trumpet

There is a current uprising among military veterans—not to the pitchfork and flaming torch stage yet, but turbulent nonetheless—regarding the recently authorized methods for playing "Taps" at military funerals. It seems that there aren't enough buglers to go around, so the Powers-that-Be decided that electronic bugles and taped recordings will suffice.

The Powers-that-Be, in case you haven't noticed, are good at making bad decisions, and here is a case in point. In fact, this is such a stinker of a policy that it inspired a fellow named Tom Day to start an outfit in 2000 that he calls Bugles Across America. Mr. Day believes that veterans deserve to have "Taps" played in person when they are laid to rest.

So now more than 5,000 buglers, in all fifty states, rebuild donated bugles, polish them up, then volunteer to attend the last rites of veterans—people they don't even know—and play "Taps." Which is, a bugle-playing acquaintance assures me, a particularly difficult piece to render.

I'm all in favor of Bugles Across America, and encourage you to visit its Web site—buglesacrossamerica.org—especially if you have an old bugle in the attic and know how to coax a tune out of it.

Recently, I saw firsthand how powerful the playing of that little ditty can be.

My Uncle Arch Iddings was a veteran of two wars—Korea

and Vietnam—flew fighter jets, was a test pilot, served as the senior air force liaison to the American embassy in London, and was a short-list finalist, early in his stint, in the Mercury astronaut program. He retired twenty-five or so years ago as a full colonel, serving at the time in the Pentagon. I think you would agree that he had a stellar career.

I was the ring bearer when he married my mother's sister in 1957 and was the eulogist at his funeral a few weeks ago. He loved his family (and I proudly count myself as a recipient of that particular blessing), and he loved to read. So we had much to talk about when we got together, and I miss him.

At the conclusion of his funeral, an honor detail from Barksdale Air Force Base paid a final tribute to him on behalf of, as one of the airmen said as he presented the flag to the family, "the president of the United States and a grateful nation." It made for some somber moments in that old cemetery in Livingston when those young people in their razor-sharp dress blues marched in perfect precision, folded that flag into a tight triangle, and fired a twenty-one gun salute. But what brought a lump to my throat and a tear to my eye was when a lone bugler stood apart on a slight rise and played "Taps."

That little detail goes to lots of funerals these days, I imagine. Mostly of young people who were killed in the current conflict, or of old ones—like Uncle Arch—who were veterans of old wars. But if the rituals they perform regularly have become old hat for them they didn't show it. When that bugler played that sacred song, it was obvious that every note was heartfelt.

My crack research team—Google.com—tells me that there are no official words to "Taps." But the first stanza of the traditional lyrics that have wandered down the years are these: "Day is done, gone the sun, from the hills, from the lake, from the skies. All is well, safely rest, God is nigh."

I thought of those words that day, as the slow, mournful series of notes lifted up through the tall pine trees on that hilltop. And I could almost sense the good man that was my uncle rising with them. It was a fine conclusion to a shining career and a life well-lived.

Everyone in the military who makes the ultimate sacrifice for this country, and everyone who gave long years of distinguished service to it, deserves every tribute that we are capable of bestowing. And that includes the playing of "Taps" by a real person on a real bugle. It has been this nation's way of sending its honored dead off to God for well over a century. And it still should be.

No matter what the cost. No matter what the inconvenience. Period.

Make mine with mayo,
and pile on the onions

What's your favorite sandwich? Quick. The first response to questions like that is usually the correct one.

I'm of the opinion that a person's favorite sandwich says a lot about who they really are. Elvis Presley's, as you are probably already aware, was banana and peanut butter. Dagwood Bumstead's is either one of his towering, multi-layered concoctions or, when he's less ravenous, mashed potato. My mother's was a big slab of purple onion and plenty of ketchup. When our daughters were little girls, they put potato chips inside their sandwiches, a procedure for which I could never see the benefit, since the chips made more sense, to me, as a side order. But, to each his own. The composition of sandwiches is an entirely personal affair.

Of course, your selection might depend on whatever mood you are currently in. In *Moving On*, a novel by Larry McMurtry, Patsy, his heroine—or villain; opinions vary—is a constant inventor of new sandwiches, her creations reflecting her ever-changing disposition.

I can relate to that. On some days, my favorite sandwich is sweet pickle, cheese and mayo. Other days, nothing else will do but a thick slab of good ham slathered in hot mustard. I used to have days when I wouldn't be satisfied until I had a pickle loaf sandwich, but I finally came to terms with the fact that there are just too many mysteries surrounding the ingredients in pickle loaf, not to mention the lofty numbers regarding triglycerides, cholesterol, and fat.

Speaking of fat. There's just not much better, some days, than a sliced brisket sandwich with enough fat still on board to make it worth the plunge and enough onions to make you keep your distance from other folks for a while.

Much of the time, a big Reuben is a good candidate for my favorite, if the sauerkraut is sufficiently sour and the corned beef is spicy. I build a particularly good one—if I do say so myself—and sear it to buttery, crisp-edged perfection in a hot skillet.

A BLT has to be in the running. The one they serve at the 59 Diner in Houston would make any cardiologist's zero tolerance list, since they manage to shove about a half a pound of crisp bacon in there, making it a chore to lift up and negotiate.

And I can't possibly leave out either egg salad (my cousin Suzy up at Canyon Lake makes one with chopped bacon that is so good it should be illegal) or a fried egg sandwich on toast. When I was in the army in Germany, several of us who were of such low rank that we had no club to go to would knock on the kitchen door of the NCO club and pay the cook to make fried egg sandwiches for us. He pocketed all the cash himself of course, which was OK with us. Walking back across that little base to our barracks on frigid winter nights, we'd cling tight to those warm, foil-wrapped parcels, anticipating how fine they'd taste with the dark local beer already chilling on the windowsill.

Well, we started out with me asking you what your favorite sandwich was, and I spent most of our time today talking about my own preferences. Which is generally how it goes here. Forgive me; sandwiches rank pretty high with me.

Sometimes just watching Spencer Tracy eat one in an old movie makes me hungry. He was the best eater of sandwiches in the history of the cinema, no question. In film after film he'd plop heavily down, spread butter on slices of bread, carefully lay on meat and cheese with the precision of a surgeon, and then obviously savor each slow bite, rubbing his hand across the bottom of his leathery face. Mr. Tracy has cost me more than a few late night visits to the kitchen.

The most popular story of the origin of this culinary art form affords the honor to the Earl of Sandwich, who supposedly didn't want to leave a hot card game to eat, so he had a servant slap some meat between two pieces of bread.

That old tale, of course, is probably about as factual as Mrs. O'Leary's cow kicking over the lantern that started the big Chicago fire.

But, if the Earl did make the first one, he has my gratitude.

And, speaking of Chicago, I had a Chicago Italian beef sandwich once that might have to be added to my list.

A short stay

Imagine, if you please, a timeline. You know, one of those horizontal graphs that you might have seen on the wall in history class that showed that the storming of the Bastille occurred about the same time that George Washington was sworn in as the first president, and that Boston's Fenway Park opened on the same day that the Titanic sank. Fenway Park is still being used; the Bastille, George Washington and the Titanic are all gone. What have I told you about baseball? It's a keeper.

Anyway, back to that timeline. And I'm talking about an all-inclusive one, everything from the first humans—Garden of Eden, boiling prehistoric sea, intergalactic visitation; it's your call and we'll steer clear of that can of worms—to however long life on this planet will last before we blow ourselves up or the sun fizzles out and the curtain comes down.

It's a concrete fact—a real lead-pipe cinch—that my time here, and yours, won't take up much space on that graph.

It's none of my business what you believe in regards to an afterlife: heaven, nirvana, rebirth as a marigold, or turn out the lights, the party's over. Whatever any of us expect or hope for later, one glance at that timeline and you've got to know that our individual time here is a swift bit of business.

People who know about such things have determined that the average human lifespan a century from now might be around 115 years. But even that long ride won't amount to much more than a raindrop in the ocean in the vast, grand scheme of things.

Now, before we get all maudlin here, let me get to the point. Which you will be happy to finally get to, I suspect.

It seems to me that, given our short visit, we'd do well to make the best of the time that we do have. Wasting life, down to the very hours and minutes of it, seems like high folly when you consider how little of it is allotted. And I feel more than a little ashamed when I whine about trivial inconveniences and then see interviews with people like Elizabeth Edwards, who is terminally ill. No matter what you think about her husband's politics or his presidential chances, you have to admit that she is one determined, courageous woman.

Instead of calling it quits and moping about the raw deal she got, she keeps a daily schedule that would wear out healthy people, and she spends as much time with her family as she can. She says, in those interviews, that she looks at everything as if for the first time, not the last.

In *Mr. Smith Goes to Washington* the character played by Jimmy Stewart says people ought to try to see everything like they're coming out of a tunnel. You know that feeling, when the bright world slaps you in the face, sort of like Dorothy opening the door of her bleak, black and white farmhouse and having to squint at the Technicolor bombardment of Oz.

I think that's how Elizabeth Edwards and many others like her must look at life. If I end up in that situation—standing on the very edge of eternity—I only hope I can look at things that way.

I respectfully submit that this whole affair needs to be viewed in terms of quality, not quantity. Odds are that you know people who have packed more living into two or three decades than many, many others have into eight or nine.

When folks like Elizabeth Edwards pass away, you can be sure that they used up all of life, in spite of the fact that it wasn't long enough. And for someone who spends all of it—filling it up daily with something useful and hopeful—life never is long enough.

I once knew a woman in East Texas who refused to waste one bit of her time worrying about death. She was almost ninety when I saw her, one nice afternoon, planting a tree sapling in her side yard.

She wiped her brow and explained that it was an oak.

"An oak makes fine shade," she told me.

So, when I get gloomy, and start weighing the brevity of human life, I think of that woman planting a shade tree that she would never sit under.

She filled her little speck on the timeline brimming full and made it count for something.

You want equality?
Build a town dump

So there I was, dragging this mass of interlocked branches and foliage to the curb, like Will Smith lugging the alien across the desert in *Independence Day*. The overgrown hedge hadn't looked nearly so huge, or intimidating, when I began hacking away at it. But by the time I was half way to the street with it I think it had actually grown. Like kudzu.

Back when I was a knobby-kneed, crewcut lad in East Texas, stuff like that hedge wouldn't have been dragged out to the curb. In fact, we didn't have a curb. Our yard sloped down to a bar ditch beside Highway 79 a little south of Oakwood. And if you put brush or garbage out there it would either rot in place or get pulverized by an eighteen-wheeler that veered too far to starboard. But nothing you put out there would get collected by a garbage truck. Because Oakwood didn't have one.

What we did have was a town dump. It was located way up a steep dirt road that ran by Dunbar, the school for black children. It also ran close by the home and front room business of a certain bootlegger who conducted a thriving business.

The dump was a wide, deep pit at the top of the hill where everybody just tossed in their garbage. It stank like nobody's business, as you can imagine, and even the trees that towered over it looked putrid and sickly. An abundance of crows congregated there constantly, and you could hear their demonic cawing on foggy mornings even before you saw the place itself. All in all, that hilltop was a bleak enough setting that Mr. Edgar Allan Poe might have made good use of it. In fact, it was the place that I envisioned when I was told, in Sunday School, about the wretched place of stoning outside the city gates of Jerusalem.

But, ironically, when I look back at it from the perspective offered by an abundance of time, I've come to think that the town dump was, even though physically grotesque, more enlightened than we gave it credit for. It was completely democratic, with a small d—not to be confused with Democratic with a capital D, which described very nearly every registered voter thereabouts.

It didn't matter if you rented a tumble-down wooden shack down by the railroad track or if you owned a quarter of the acreage in the county, your trash went in with everyone else's. And it was entirely your responsibility to get it there.

The families of the kids that attended Dunbar threw their garbage in the same big pile as those whose children went to the white school.

The local laundromat was segregated. So were all the churches and the Melba movie theater. Laurene's Café had a separate dining room behind the kitchen for black people, with its own entrance. We all ate identical hamburgers and "dinner plates"—slices of roast beef or fried steak with a mound of mashed potatoes and English peas and a dollop of fruit salad in the exact center—but common consensus dictated that we had to eat it in different rooms.

Even Dr. Bell's office in Palestine, where I went to get prodded and jabbed when I got sick, had a waiting room that was divided by a half wall; one side for white patients, the other for blacks. I tried to peek around that wall once to see if black children read a different version of *Highlights for Children*.

Then, as a final assertion of wrong-minded but deeply entrenched tradition, black people were buried in an entirely different cemetery, just down the hill from the white one. Two plots of sacred ground separated by a fence that I'm confident isn't in place in whatever the hereafter has to offer.

Like every little southern burg back then, practically every-thing was segregated. Except for the town dump. And, ugly and smelly as it was, it silently served as a precursor, a harbinger pointing the way to better days ahead.

It's funny how repulsive things or people can serve useful functions like that, don't you think? It holds out hope for every ugly and frightful creature, person, or thing in creation.

Now, after all of that, it occurs to me that we wouldn't have hauled a hacked-up hedge to the dump anyway. We would have piled it up behind the house and burned it. But let's save the burning of leaves and bushes for cooler weather. Something that nostalgic will play better after the first strong norther blows through.

The quiet man
at the helm
of a noisy place

We always thought he looked like Dick Clark. He even seemed to be immune to the aging process like Dick Clark was, as if they weren't really human. But what Gene Marcum really looked like was a principal.

He was, in fact, what I thought every principal ought to look like. In my opinion and countless others, he was the gold standard of principals.

I first met him on a hot summer day in 1981. I had taught and coached in three school districts in four years when I got a call from the athletic director of a district south of Houston, who said they needed a tennis coach–English teacher combination. He wanted to know if I would drive down and discuss it with him and the principal. What he meant, of course, was that they wanted to get a good look at me; they were both old school men and put as much value on first impressions as on resumes.

I had just moved away from the Gulf Coast and hadn't planned on returning to it. But I made that trip, and we all must have liked the looks of each other. I agreed to sign a one-year contract.

Then Mr. Marcum reached into his desk and took out two narrow strips of paper, saying there was only one little transaction that we had to conclude before he would okay the deal. So I purchased my first tickets to the Rotary Club Shrimp Boil, an event for which he was the chairman that year.

Outside, he told me he was glad to have me on board and I confided in him that I was pretty much of a wanderer.

"I'll probably only stay a year or two," I told him. "Then I'll move on."

He smiled that little smile that I would come to know awfully well.

"I'll bet against that," he said. "I'll bet you're here to stay."

That was going on twenty-seven years ago. So he was right.

He usually was, in just about every situation.

My friend, Frank Curl, who hired on when I did in another high school in the district, recalls seeing him do what he did best once. It was at some big event and one of our students was misbehaving, and being loud about it, as students are apt to do on occasion. Whereupon Mr. Marcum stepped slowly over and had a quiet word with the kid. And he stopped his shenanigans. It was as simple as that.

Frank, now an assistant principal, was impressed by that. If he had been around him constantly, like I was, he would have been used to it. Because he had a knack for diffusing little situations before they could grow into bigger ones. Just like he had one for earning respect without really going out of his way to work for it.

In all the years I worked for him, I'll bet I saw him without a necktie on less than five times. And I heard him raise his voice even fewer times than that. Another principal I once worked for used to raise his pretty often, throwing little tantrums at faculty meetings and yelling at kids like a banshee. He lost his effectiveness and his faculty's respect quickly; Mr. Marcum maintained both throughout his career.

That serene, laid-back philosophy could be aggravating at times. His standard response to most questions—regarding budget items, field trip requests, or just about anything that he had to sign off on—was "I'll get back to you."

The problem was that he very often never did. And, in retrospect, I imagine he dealt with the major things and let the minor ones just disappear. "I'll get back to you" was his version of a pocket veto.

I've thought of him a lot this past week, this fine man, fine husband and father, and fine principal who looked so much like Dick Clark.

Because, like Dick Clark—who suffered a massive stroke a few years ago—he finally turned out to be human after all.

He wandered slowly into the sad shadow land of Alzheimer's and, last Saturday, he slipped away completely. And what a loss for all of us who knew and loved him.

God bless you, Mr. Marcum. On behalf of your teachers and students—numbering in the thousands—thank you for being the steady, gentle landmark that we had foolishly convinced ourselves would never change.

The Maugham problem

When somebody tells me about a book or a movie they enjoyed that offered pure escapism—no deep hidden themes, no grandiose symbolism or social instruction—I'm reminded of one of my favorite authors, W. Somerset Maugham. He always followed a simple rule. He believed the job of the writer is to tell a good story and not to enlighten, educate, or reshape the world.

He spun excellent yarns for sixty-five years. When his first book, *Liza of Lambeth*, was published in 1897, his contemporaries were H. G. Wells, Rudyard Kipling, and Thomas Hardy. When he penned his last one, *Purely for Pleasure*, in 1962, his competition included John Updike and J. D. Salinger. I can't think of another writer whose work spanned such a full sweep of time.

He stayed too long as a playwright. His witty Edwardian social dramas, heralded in the first years of the twentieth century as the finest in London and New York, paled in comparison to the angrier, meatier plays of Tennessee Williams, Arthur Miller, and many others.

But his stories and his novels have held up nicely. Most of his work is still in print, some titles having surpassed their centennials already. *The Moon and Sixpence* and *Cakes and Ale* were as enjoyable and as moving on my second reading of them as they were on my first, back when I was in college and was impressed with practically any book handed to me.

Maugham's life was both pleasant and tortured, not an uncommon mixture for artistic people. He made his entire living by his pen—literally so; he never used a typewriter and made his exit before the advent of personal computers—and he lived well. But his personal life was pretty much a disaster. At the end of it he had outlived most of his family and friends, and alienated the ones who were left.

And there was what came to be known as "The Maugham Problem," which involved the discrepancy between the fact that he was not considered by most eminent critics and scholars to be in the top echelon of English writers, and the verifiable reality that he was the most popular author since Dickens. His works were translated into most languages, many of them were made and remade into successful movies—the most recent version of *The Painted Veil* came out just last year—and he had quietly become, at the time of his death, the highest paid writer of fiction in history. An honor recently laid claim to by J. K. Rowling.

Maugham accepted his limitations and saw himself in the "very first row of the second-raters." According to his best biographer, Ted Morgan: "all his life he would suffer from the sense that he was cut off from genius, and that he stood on a hillock in the lowlands and would never go higher."

But maybe the final victory was his after all. He managed to outlive all those critics and scholars and, through pure persistence and prolific production, to become the grand old man of English letters. He must have been disappointed to be passed over annually for the Nobel Prize in Literature—especially when it was given, for political reasons, to lesser talents – but he just as surely had to have felt vindicated when he sat, ancient and world-famous (the *Life* magazine photo of him at Grace Kelly's marriage to Prince Rainier was larger, even, than the one of the newlyweds) in his grand villa on the Mediterranean and gazed at the long row of his published works on the shelf.

The "Maugham Problem" raises an important question: just who should an author write for? The many levels of everyday folk who go about their daily lives and look to books and stories for entertainment? Or the meticulous scholars who dissect every nuance and phrasing and judge writing by criteria that the general reading public knows little about and cares even less for?

W. Somerset Maugham should have had his Nobel Prize. Furthermore, he should have been buried in the Poet's Corner in Westminster Abbe, in the company of Chaucer, Dickens, and T. S. Eliot.

But, on second thought, maybe where he ended up in 1965 is even better. He asked to have his ashes interred on the grounds of the King's School at Canterbury, where he had spent several unhappy years as a stuttering schoolboy. There, in the shade of the cathedral that was the destination of Chaucer's storytelling pilgrims is what Maugham's biographer calls "a fitting burial place for a teller of tales."

A dark night,
a chilly room,
and a ghost

Around about now, interest runs high regarding spirits and goblins and things that go bump in the night. Pumpkins—some carved, most not—adorn lots of front porches and little black and orange ghosts dangle from more than a few trees in my neighborhood. When a slight breeze kicks up, those ghosts flutter and dance enough to make me think of the only actual ghost that I might have ever come in contact with.

That would be the Ghost of Brazoswood.

I hadn't been on the payroll at that particular high school more than fifteen minutes—way back in 1981—before at least two people had told me about her.

And the common consensus is that it is a "her." Which really makes the ghost all the more enticing. And romantic. The most popular tale is that she was a young lady who lived on the plantation that once included the land where the school would later be built—over a century later, in fact. It seems that she fell in love, got engaged, and was left standing at the altar by some rapscallion who apparently didn't become a ghost, at least not one who hung around the vicinity. Because it's not him that is the subject of stories, generation after generation.

It is her.

Some people say she committed suicide. Others maintain she died of a broken heart. One yarn has her living into very old age, never once leaving the house in which she was to have been married, never again taking off her wedding dress.

But even if she lived to be a hundred (if she lived at all) it is not an old woman that people report seeing on occasion; it is a beautiful young lady in a bright white dress.

One janitor that still worked at the school when I started there swore that he was sweeping on the second floor landing beside a stairwell late one night when, upon turning around, he stood face to face with Her Ghostliness—or whatever you call a specter—as she floated in mid-air over the stairs.

He was a soft-spoken gentleman given to understatement, when I asked him about it, he said only that it had certainly gotten his attention.

Teachers who have to go there at night to get lesson plans ready for a substitute or run off tests are pretty much in agreement that it's a little eerie. Many say they have felt her presence there. And one old friend who shall remain nameless says he sometimes catches himself stepping a little faster than usual to get to an exit.

There's no evidence that our ghost has ever done anything malicious. If she's really there, she's just hanging around. Maybe she can't leave, which would be sad. Or maybe she just refuses to move on to wherever she is supposed to be, which might even be sadder.

Now, for that encounter that I might—or might not—have had with her.

It was a dark, cold night (of course; why would it be anything else? This is a ghost story, remember) and I had just brought a busload of my tennis players back from a match way down in Victoria. While they were in the gym office calling their parents to come collect them (this was long before cell phones), I took our tennis balls and medical kit to the little storage room on the other side of the gym.

I never knew where the light switch was in that big gym, so I just aimed in the direction of the opposite door. It was pitch dark and breath vapor cold. I got the stuff stowed away and, on the return trip, I actually felt, in the middle of the gym floor, a presence. Then, something knocked against my tennis shoe. Then something else. Then another something.

Needless to say, I made a hasty exit. The next morning I found, in the middle of the gym floor, three basketballs that the coach assured me had been put away in a hopper by the wall.

I once told this story to someone who studies such goings-on and she just nodded a very knowing nod. Spirits are attracted to cold places, she told me, and they are particularly comfortable in empty schools. Where else, she asked me, is there that much frantic, youthful energy during the day, and an absolute absence of it at night? Ghosts, she said, like the remnants of energy.

None of this is by way of saying that I believe in ghosts. Or that one provided the three love taps that night in that gym.

But something did.

Mr. Handy Man

There are fifty-eight cabinet knobs in my kitchen.

I know this because my wife and I spent a chunk of the summer giving that chamber and the adjacent breakfast and laundry rooms a makeover.

I know this, also, because I removed all fifty-eight of the original knobs, replaced them with brand new ones after the cabinets and drawers were all sanded and painted, and then removed those and replaced them because that aforementioned wife didn't like the looks of the ones she originally chose.

This refurbishing was a big chore. First, we stripped off all the old wallpaper, an odd pattern of what we sometimes thought were little detached birds' wings and sometimes feathers that had been in place since the house was built. Then, we had to sand the seams of the paper's backing which had adhered itself to the wall with sufficient tenacity to render any attempt at removal doomed from the outset. After that we slapped (in my case) and carefully brushed (in Karen's) on a heavy coat of Kilz, a globular paint thick enough to cover past sins and lapses in good taste. Next, we painted the ceiling, painted it again, applied a coat of texture to the walls and, finally, spread on a couple of coats of a soft, golden hue called Ripe Wheat.

I pretty much followed Karen's lead and sanded where I was told to sand and painted where I was told to paint.

She had better sense than to let me loose with oil-based paint, which she used on the cabinets and drawers. And that was certainly fine with me. During the two days that she undertook that delicate procedure, I kept company with Will, Grace, Earl Gray, and Missy, our quartet of cats who were sequestered in the master bedroom so they wouldn't add their own brushstrokes.

The plan was for me to settle into the comfortable chair in there and get some writing done on my laptop computer. But the bill of fare on the American Movie Classics channel was too enticing, so the cats and I ended up watching one old movie after another.

After all the paint had dried and the drop cloths were folded up, Karen let it be known that her part of the project was done, and that, in the division of labors, the installation of anything electrical fell into my territory.

I need to make a confession about now.

You could randomly select any ten men my age and it's a safe bet that at least eight of them would be better at installing, tinkering with, or repairing things around the house than yours truly. It's just not my thing. Power tools hold no fascination for me, and a workshop in my garage would be an absolute waste of space.

When I was a boy at church camp one summer I built my mother a birdhouse that was so lopsided and grotesque that even she—who taped my drawings on the refrigerator long before the advent of those cute little magnets—conveniently misplaced it.

I'm not quite so inept that I'd consider buying a new lamp when the bulb goes out. But I'm not far from it. Suffice it to say, Mr. Fix-It I am not.

At least I wasn't until this summer, when I somehow managed to install four medium-sized light fixtures, a sprawling hanging fixture over the breakfast table, a new security light on the garage, and a new vent fan and hood over the range. I accomplished all of this without electrocuting myself or knocking big holes in the walls. Though I do admit that the hanging fixture and I squared off in a desperate battle which it darn near won. My blood pressure skyrocketed that morning, and Karen decided it was her turn to spend a little quality time with the cats. And away from me.

Had I, when I returned to my school a few weeks later, been asked to write an essay about what I did on my summer vacation (there's really no telling what one might be asked to do in a teacher in-service meeting) I would have related how I found a part of myself that I'd never realized was there. Sort of an old dog/new tricks epiphany.

If ever, God forbid, I find myself stranded on the Sahara like those guys in *Flight of the Phoenix*, I might not be able to build an aircraft out of parts left over from the one that crashed and fly us all to safety. But, should we need a vent hood installed out there, I'll be the guy for the job.

The best laid plans
of rice and hen

Here's a cautionary tale about making plans and following them. It involves seven people, a big RV, and a sizable portion of the continental United States.

Our chariot was luxury itself. It had plenty of space, a galley, comfortable seating, a bathroom and shower, two televisions, a state-of-the-art stereo system, a variety of good wine in the rack, a queen-sized bed in the back, and it floated along on a cushion of air. It was the favorite plaything of my brother-in-law, Thomas, and was a real dandy, that rig. I felt like Captain Kirk at the helm of the *Enterprise* in the plush captain's seat with the sprawling windshield offering a panoramic view in front of me. Of course, I wasn't allowed to actually drive such an expensive contraption. But Captain Kirk didn't actually drive the *Enterprise*, either. Now, did he?

We were seven, as I said. And we made that trip in stages, sort of like the different phases of one of NASA's trips to the moon back in the days when we ventured out more often.

In stage one, my wife Karen and my two sisters, Janie and Diane, along with our cousin Suzy flew from Dallas to Jackson Hole, Wyoming. My brother-in-law Thomas and Suzy's husband Dave and I drove, in the RV, to Taos, New Mexico. Then we wound through Colorado, up through Utah and Idaho, and over into Wyoming, where we joined the girls in Jackson Hole and Yellowstone. At night, Janie and Thomas got the RV; the rest of us put up in cabins. After a few days, we crawled back on board and crossed Wyoming into South Dakota, where we did Mount Rushmore and the Black Hills before heading home.

For that trip, the plan was that we would do chef duty for two nights each. That way, we—good cooks all—could trot out our specialties. And, even more important, if we each cooked twice, then we wouldn't be paying for expensive chow at restaurants. So, before we left, the girls made up complete menus for what promised to be a cross-country epicurean odyssey.

Thomas would grill thick rib-eyes twice, with baked potatoes the size of softballs. One night we'd have a plump hen, roasted in a bed of savory brown rice. One of my offerings would be chili. I'm a good hand at chili, my secret—that is, until now—being boiling browned beef in stout beer before adding in the rest of the fixings.

Somebody was supposed to cook a pot of turnip greens one night, to go along with a big skillet full of corn bread. All of us had grown up eating country food, most of it fresh from the garden, and that pot of greens seemed like a fine idea.

But, as we progressed through our journey, local fare like fresh mountain trout, corn-fed Nebraska beef, fried potatoes and huckleberry pie sang us a different song. And, like Odysseus' sailors lured in by the evil sirens, we plopped down at one restaurant table after another, running up our cholesterol, our weights, and our credit card balances.

When that trip was over, we hadn't cooked one single thing in that RV other than a frozen casserole that Thomas, Dave and I heated up in the parking lot of a Wal-Mart in Pocatello, Idaho. When it became apparent, near the end of the two weeks, that I wouldn't be making the chili after all, I drank the beer I'd brought along for that purpose. Waste not; want not.

So all our planning amounted to nothing, in the end.

But one plan that I made, having nothing to do with food, did actually come to fruition at the very end of our voyage.

I had packed a CD of the soundtrack for the movie *Giant*, and when we crossed the Red River and slipped out of Oklahoma into the Lone Star state, I put that CD in and turned the volume up to blasting for "This is Texas!" That piece is one stirring bit of business, and all of us native-born Texans—except for Dave, who was born in Missouri but has lived down here long enough to be accorded honorary status—felt sufficiently proud and moved as we made our triumphant homecoming.

My sister Diane even cried a little. Which surprised nobody; Diane is a crier. She's also one of the best cooks I've ever known. Though you certainly wouldn't have known it on that trip.

Acknowledgments

I am grateful to Bill Cornwell, my friend and my annual lunch companion, for launching this project, to Yvonne Mintz, the managing editor at the paper, and to Glenn Krampota, the features editor, to Judy Alter and Susan Petty, at TCU Press, for seeing enough potential in these weekly offerings for a book, and to my friends and neighbors who actually read these things on Sunday mornings.

I owe most of my gratitude to Karen, my wife and my best friend, who graciously allows me to splash our shared life out in the paper more often than most wives would be happy about.

About the Author

Ron Rozelle, besides writing a weekly column in the *Brazosport Facts*, is the author of six books—three novels, two memoirs, and a *Writer's Digest* volume on description and setting. A member of the Texas Institute of Letters, he teaches creative writing and senior English in high school and conducts memoir and fiction workshops around the country. *Into that Good Night*, his memoir about growing up in east Texas and his father's Alzheimer's ordeal, was a short list finalist for a national PEN award and was named the second best work of nonfiction in the nation in 1998 by the *San Antonio Express-News*. His novel of the 1900 Galveston hurricane, *The Windows of Heaven*, won the *Texas Review* fiction prize and the Katherine Munson Foster memorial award. He and his wife Karen live in Lake Jackson, Texas.

Sundays with Ron Rozelle
978-0-87565-390-7
Paper. $19.95

ISBN 978-0-87565-390-7

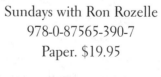

51995

9 780875 653907